MW01614845

OCCUPY

ERASE RECESSION

FUND YOUR DREAMS

CHANGE THE WORLD

JOHN
REDENBO

Writing Career Coach Press (a division of Writing Career Coach, 225 West Adrian Street, Blissfield, MI 49228) functions only as book publisher. As such, the ultimate design, content, editorial accuracy, and views expressed or implied in this work are those of the author.

Cover Art by Zakr Studio. www.zakrstudio.com

ISBN 13: 978-1-938283-01-7
ISBN 10: 1938283015

CONTENTS

Why Recession?

Have you ever asked yourself the question, Why am I here? How did I get into the financial situation I'm in? Economists in the United States and around the world have been asking that question for some time. Often, it's easy to see poor decisions we've made and the path that led us to where we are. Other times, not so much. In spite of our best efforts, many times, we find ourselves facing difficult financial challenges. For the many of us in this place, let me tell you – THERE IS HOPE!

God has a purpose behind everything that happens. Perhaps a better way of saying that is,

> *...And we know that God works all things to the good for them that love Him and are called according to His purposes...*
>
> **Romans 8:28**

With that in mind, what is the purpose of the economic conditions we see around us? Does God have a plan in recession? Not only is the answer a resounding YES, but it is also seen throughout history.

Adversity Yields Change

People don't change easily. Things continue in an inertial trend until acted on by an outside force. It's a law of physics and human nature. We see many times in the Bible God calling his people up, to a higher level. In His incredible mercy and desire for us not to stay stuck or stagnant, our Father shakes things up to get our attention and to cause needed, positive change. Economic recession was used often as far back as Biblical times as a way for God to get the attention of His people. When we are lacking economically, we cry out for help. We need a deliverer, a rescuer. That's exactly what God is counting on.

> **The cost of change, many times, is greater than we would voluntarily pay on our own, but once we're on the other side it was worth the price of admission!**

Destinies are adjusted and positions are often changed in just this way. The result of change is greater than the price of change.

- Joseph needed slavery and imprisonment to develop the character to reign in Egypt.

- Moses needed forty years in the desert prior to delivering God's people.

- Israel needed slavery to birth a nation.

- David needed training with a lion and bear to have the skill to take Goliath.

The cost of change is many times greater than we would voluntarily pay on our own, but once we're on the other side it was worth the price of admission! Recession is a change catalyst. Referred to Biblically as famine, it is employed throughout the Bible to affect movement or transformation. Famine caused Naomi and Ruth to move to a different land, leading Ruth to her Boaz, a key link in the lineage of Jesus. Drought and famine (recession) was the catalyst in Haggai that produced repentance and the completion of the temple. Recession and mortgage crisis caused change in the financial system in Israel, in Nehemiah's time, freeing the people from debt to complete the work on Jerusalem's wall.

Recession Causes Motion

Recession is designed to equal greater blessing. It gets our attention quickly. It is God communicating to His people in a

> **Recession is a change catalyst, designed to take us into greater blessing.**

language that is consistent throughout generations. He is speaking and the onus is on us to hear and act. Many times, after an adjustment or a change is made, He restores His blessing not only to us, but also to our whole land. **The power to end recession lies with us - God's people.**

So if recession is a change catalyst that God uses as a means of communicating with us, the question becomes, what is God saying? What adjustment is necessary, what higher level are we being called to, or simply, change what? What is the root or cause behind our current economic condition? Whether it's a personal recession or crisis in our own lives or a nationwide condition, the principles still apply.

I am a finance guy and I work with churches to help them find mortgages and procure funding. I became very frustrated by the downturn in the mortgage market at the beginning of 2008. I was working with a church in Florida that had been through the ringer! They had their building burnt to the ground 13 years prior and had been working on rebuilding ever since. They were several hundred thousand dollars short of what they needed to complete the project and were stuck in a loan paying twice the normal rate of interest, around 13%. What would normally have been a simple 60-day process stretched into 6 months. This loan was exceedingly challenging and made it very difficult to do what I know I was called to do – fund churches. Frustration, as it often does, drove me to pray. After hours a day on the phone working through issues with the new bank, the title company, attorneys, public records departments and the church, I would drop on the couch at the end of the day irritated and wondering if we were ever going to get this project the money they needed.

During those times of prayer, I would speak very plainly to God about the challenges, and I could hear Him answer me. We had this inner dialogue going that went like this:

God - "What's the problem, son?"

Me - "Well God, it's like this; we have to get waivers of lien release on every contractor that touched this building in the last 13 years so the loan can clear title."

God - "What's title work?"

Me - "You see God, it's like this; when we lend money to a church, we have to make sure the property is free of any other liens or claims to the property so we can place our lien on it."

God - "Why do you need liens?"

Me - "Well God, if the Pastor doesn't pay us back the money he owes us, we can take his church away."

God - "...oh...that's not how I would do it..."

Me - "...uh, ok God... How would you do it?"

God - "Go back to the original model."

Me - "What model? No offense God, but 'the borrower is a slave to the lender?' What is that? Something out of a fortune cookie?!"

(Again, please remember, I was pretty frustrated!)

God - "Go back to the original model." Transmission ends...

What model?

I had never seen a Biblical model for financing churches. I frankly, had serious doubts that there was anything in Scripture that would help on a practical level. We've all heard people talk about running from debt and buying things in cash, but in cases of building a church, it's very near impossible! At least it certainly was in this case! That didn't mean there wasn't a Biblical model.

The reason a craftsman has a pattern or model is so they have a consistent way of fabricating something. If they didn't have one, they would have to make a copy of a copy of a copy. Have you ever seen a faxed copy? It's grainy and hard to read. Imagine a fax of a copy of a copy! The point is, the further removed from the pattern you get, the less recognizable is the end result. At some point what we have left is so different from what we started with that we forgot what the original model is supposed to even look like.

Going back to the original can tell you a lot about the design and function. You can see why the master craftsman made things a certain way when you see the parts fitting together and operating perfectly. It's difficult with a copy to determine what went wrong and where. Making adjustments and corrections can seem laborious until we go back to the original and adjust according to the pattern.

There are many patterns to discover in the Bible if you are tuned in to them and seeking them out. For example, recession is often used as a precursor to great blessing and even outpouring, repositioning and promotion. A dramatic,

> **The reason craftsmen have a pattern or model is so they have a consistent way of fabricating something... Going back to the original can tell you a lot about the design and function.**

severe famine and depressed economic situation, many times, preceded a major building event such as the building of the tabernacle, the rebuilding of the temple and the rebuilding of the wall of Jerusalem. Biblical models show us what the patterns look like and how we may need to adjust our way of thinking.

Transformation

*Do not conform any longer to the patterns of this
world, but be transformed, by the renewing of your
minds.*

Romans 12:2

Transformation – is a buzzword we hear all the time in Christian circles;
transforming missions, transforming lives, transforming churches,
communities, nations and the world. But where is it **truly** happening?
There are pockets of transformation, pieces here and there. When a
location begins to experience "revival" and people are healed, signs and
wonders happen, we pack up our RVs and head to Toronto, Brownsville,
Lakeland or wherever. But does revival or transformation occur only in
specific areas?

Transformation is not a place we visit, it is a place we live! To
transform means *to change, transfigure; to change in form, appearance
or structure, to change in condition, nature or character.* It comes
from the Greek word "metamorphoo" which literally means to
metamorphose.

So since we know that recession is a key way in which God
communicates with His people that change is needed, and we know that
renewing our minds brings change or transformation, the question
becomes, in what areas do we need to make our minds new? Let's ask
some tough questions:

- Is the mission model we have today getting the job done?

- Is the church in America thriving and growing?

- Do we have a vibrant presence globally that is transforming cities and communities around the world?

- Why is it that only 1 out of 20 people who claim to be Christians will ever lead someone else to the Lord?

Let's go a little deeper;

- Are the models of churches and ministries we have today producing disciples?

- Are the experiences we have in church even designed to transform us?

- Why is it that Jesus, with a rag-tag group of 12 men, could prepare them in **three years** to be the leaders of a movement that still exists today and yet most of us have been in churches that long with no noticeable change at all?

- Where is the transforming power of the Gospel?

When I look at the economic condition of the church, I hear that half a billion dollars worth of churches are in default or foreclosure, revenues are declining pretty much across the board, missionaries are being furloughed and sent home as their support wanes, and ministries are shutting their doors and closing down everyday. Should that be getting our attention? Is God trying to tell us something?

The news is not all bad. There are places where the Gospel is thriving. People are experiencing healing, disciples are being made, as ministry is happening and even multiplying. But with all the technology we have today, have you ever stopped and thought, "Why doesn't the whole world know about Jesus yet?"

> **With all the technology we have today, have you ever stopped and thought, "Why doesn't the whole world know about Jesus yet?**

When consulting with businesses or organizations, it is always helpful to see the problems that exist and then move to a place where we identify constraints. So why are churches in foreclosure? Why are missionaries being sent home? Why are ministries closing their doors and dying? Why hasn't the Gospel been more advanced in America and overseas than it is? Why don't we have ongoing revival? Why not transformation?

I have asked these questions of others and of myself. Many times the conclusion is the same – lack: a lack of financial support, a lack of lenders to lend to churches, a lack of giving units, revenue and resources. Many times it seems like that answer comes down to simply not having enough-- enough people to volunteer, enough money to fund outreach, missions, programs, staff, etc.

We have all heard, "There is no lack in God's Kingdom." Nice thought, experientially though, there seems to be a huge disconnect between the churches I am working with to save from foreclosure and that statement. The cold hard truth is many churches are experiencing lack. The question then becomes WHY?

As we discussed, recession is a change catalyst. It brings people into alignment with God and His will. We see it over and over again in Scripture, how His people would experience exile, famine, war – LACK. Then He would send a prophet or a judge to tell the people of their mistake and how to correct it. In almost every situation, repentance was involved. Repentance simply means "changing your mind" or "going in a different direction".

It's amazing to me how many people have been through programs designed to help them in their finances. Many of them go back several times and still are not debt free or doing much better than they were the first time. How many people go on diets and may even lose weight, but gain it back? This is not just a church problem; we see it prevalent in many places.

> **How can Christians sit in church year after year and still struggle with the same problems in their marriages, finances and personal lives? The short answer is – transformation is not occurring.**

Recidivism (convicts returning to prison for repeat offenses) is one of the main problems with our justice system. Why is it that after spending years incarcerated, a person will return after once again gaining their freedom? Good question! How can Christians sit in church year after year and still struggle with the same problems in their marriages, finances and personal lives? After all, we're supposed to have the answers, right???

The short answer is – transformation is not occurring. If we are to be transformed by the renewing of our minds, then the root of the problem may very well be that our minds are not being renewed. To renew is *to make new again, to turn from the old and embrace the new*. It's interesting that as I write, I am thinking of the verse where God is telling us, "My thoughts are not your thoughts..." When I look this up, I find the following:

An Invitation to Abundant Life

Ho! Everyone who thirsts,
Come to the waters;
And you who have no money,
Come, buy and eat.
Yes, come, buy wine and milk,
Without money and without price.
Why do you spend money for what is not bread,
And your wages for what does not satisfy?
Listen carefully to Me, and eat what is good,
And let your soul delight itself in abundance.
Incline your ear, and come to Me.
Hear, and your soul shall live;
And I will make an everlasting covenant with you—
The sure mercies of David.
Indeed I have given him as a witness to the people,
A leader and commander for the people.
Surely you shall call a nation you do not know,
And nations who do not know you shall run to you,
Because of the LORD your God,
And the Holy One of Israel;
For He has glorified you."

Seek the LORD while He may be found,
Call upon Him while He is near.

Let the wicked forsake his way,
And the unrighteous man his thoughts;
Let him return to the LORD,
And He will have mercy on him;
And to our God,
For He will abundantly pardon.

"For My thoughts are not your thoughts,
Nor are your ways My ways," says the LORD.
"For as the heavens are higher than the earth,
So are My ways higher than your ways,
And My thoughts than your thoughts.

"For as the rain comes down, and the snow from heaven,
And do not return there,
But water the earth,
And make it bring forth and bud,
That it may give seed to the sower
And bread to the eater,
So shall My word be that goes forth from My mouth;
It shall not return to Me void,
But it shall accomplish what I please,
And it shall prosper in the thing for which I sent it.

"For you shall go out with joy,
And be led out with peace;
The mountains and the hills
Shall break forth into singing before you,
And all the trees of the field shall clap their hands.
Instead of the thorn shall come up the cypress tree,
And instead of the brier shall come up the myrtle tree;
And it shall be to the LORD for a name,
For an everlasting sign that shall not be cut off."

Isaiah 55

It's amazing that in this passage where God is telling us that our
thoughts are not His thoughts, it begins with an invitation to abundant
life. "Let the wicked forsake his way and the unrighteous man his

thoughts and let him return to the Lord..." then God makes the distinction between our thoughts and His thoughts. He continues on with, "So shall My Word be that goes forth from My mouth; it shall not return to Me void, but it shall accomplish what I please, and it shall prosper in the thing for which I sent it."

The thing for which He sent it was transformation. We see it from the first chapter of the Bible where God spoke and light was created. Transformation from darkness happened. He went on to create the heavens and the earth. Initially the

> **The Word of God and the presence of God cause transformation!**

earth was "formless and void" and "the Spirit of God was hovering over the surface of the waters". He says here in Isaiah that his Word will not return void. The earth, though *formless*, was *transformed* and filled with life, plants, animals, trees, mountains, oceans, lakes, rivers, glaciers and so much more by the Word of God and the presence of God.

John 1:1 in talking about the transformation that occurred at creation says, "In the beginning was the Word and the Word was with God and the Word was God. He was with God in the beginning." The same thing (transformation) happens to us when we take in the Word of God. Because it is living and active, it changes us. It transforms us. It renews our minds and our hearts making us new. We are no longer bound to the limitations of the human condition but are free to create with God as participants in His grand plan. All that is required is that we forsake our ways and our thoughts.

So what does that look like practically? For me, it meant resolving myself to the fact that the Bible is true in every aspect, perfect, flawless and written by men inspired by God, and that it is His matchless Word. It was more than just an understanding of what I had before. The Word of God became a road map for a financial understanding that I never had before. Remember at the start of this journey, I didn't believe there was a road map or a whole lot of practical wisdom on a macroeconomic scale. But as I studied and God brought me on this journey and guided me through it, I found so many incredible principles that I have never heard before.

Once I settled the issue that the Bible does contain a financial plan, that God has a financial plan for me, churches, communities and the world, my alignment totally shifted. I began finding patterns and models in Scripture that were incredible in how they worked in Biblical times. But since I resolved the fact that the Word of God is truth, I believed there must be a way to practically implement these principles in a society that is very different.

Grace

The Word became flesh and made His dwelling among us. We have seen His glory, the glory of the one and only Son, who came from the Father, full of grace and truth.

John 1:14

This journey, searching for the "original model", began for me in early 2008 and has taken many turns. Much has happened in my life along the way that has shaped my thoughts and understanding of God. I found what an incredible financial and economic plan God has for us. I knew He had a plan, but I didn't realize the breadth and depth of that plan economically. I also saw another facet of the heart of God that was radically different from both what I had been taught and how I felt. I always held to the belief that my finances, were under my control and that when I experienced challenges they were a direct result of my poor decisions. I still believe a lot of that is true. However, it led me into the fallacy or false foundation that, because the mess I was in was my fault, I had to dig my own way out. This is a fatal trap that prevents us from looking to God as our rescuer and provider. Feeling the weight of this wasn't helpful, since I knew I didn't have the ability to speak money into existence. I needed help!

Grace Defined

The common definition of "grace" is *unearned or unmerited favor or the empowering favor of God.* The grace that is given us by our heavenly Father is exactly the same as the grace that was given to Jesus– the true empowering favor of God! The difference is that Jesus deserved it, because He was always in righteous standing with His Father.

The beautiful thing about grace is that we don't deserve it, it's our actions that put us where we are, and we are powerless, to dig our own

> **The beautiful thing about grace is that we don't deserve it!**

way out. God knows all this and He is more than willing to rescue us and provide for us even when we don't deserve it and even when it's our fault. The beauty of this truth was never more evident to me than in the last year. When this really sinks in and sticks, it is so freeing. We are not alone in our financial struggles. God cares about us and has a plan for our lives: to rescue us and bring us to a place of total fulfillment in Him.

Most of us believe that God can deliver the drug addict, set the alcoholic free, heal those who are disease ridden and transform the life of prostitutes and convicts, and yet, when it comes to our own financial mess, we resign ourselves to find our own way out. You can't save yourself anymore that a country in exile can procure its own freedom. We need God! That's the point! The presence of God and the Word of God is what brings transformation -- not our best efforts.

Under Old Testament law, when a sacrifice was brought to atone for sin, the high priest would examine it very thoroughly to make sure that it was without spot or wrinkle. The condition of the lamb ensured the acceptability of the sacrifice, not the individual whose sin was being atoned for. The killing of the lamb proved the righteousness of the one atoned for. It didn't matter what they did, what they looked like, how many times they failed, what their position was in society or how much they knew better. The condition of the person was irrelevant.

> **The condition of the lamb ensured the acceptability of the sacrifice, not the individual whose sin was being atoned for.**

That's exactly how grace is. Jesus died for all of our sins and shortcomings, whether they are big or small in our eyes or the eyes of the world. Overspending on your budget, shopping too much, too much credit card debt and the subsequent mess it creates from marital frustrations to being anxious, is all covered under the blood. Accepting it, confessing the blood of Jesus over our finances and moving forward are key parts to transforming our lives both financially and relationally with God. Changing our mindset here is also critical. We cannot rescue ourselves and it's not our job to do so – God is the rescuer. We just need to accept the work that He has already done for us.

Grace and Money

Much of the teaching in the area of finances is very self-empowered. Personal responsibility and a decent budget sheet isn't enough! The whole "pull-myself-up-by-my-bootstraps" idea, never completely resonated with me. I was responsible for the mess I was in and I knew that. I accepted responsibility for it too, but if my best efforts or inconsistencies led me to where I was, how could I change? I was the one who didn't handle my finances right in the first place, how was I going to get myself out of this mess?

The answer was simple – all I could do was accept His grace. Grace extends to the area of finances! That's the good news. God is all about rescuing us when we can't rescue ourselves. He is the ultimate Father. Even when we mess up, He is there to lift us up and provide for us. His love is never ending and His grace is infallible. The price for our redemption has been paid in full. We just need to accept it and walk in it. It's easy when you work with someone else's problems to realize that not everything in their financial world relies on them. We are not in a position to rescue ourselves since it was our bad decisions that landed us there in the first place. The light of revelation must be shone on our hearts and minds to empower us to change. Transformation always needs a catalyst and that catalyst is Jesus!

> **Transformation always needs a catalyst and that catalyst is Jesus!**

Once we recognize that we have a God who loves us and rescues us, and that our financial mistakes have been atoned for when we simply believe in Him, we become conscious of His grace in our lives. As we call out to Him and partner with Him to move forward, it becomes easier to trust Him and have a greater faith. When we're wrapped up in our problems and all of our actions that landed us there, guilt, worry, doubt and fear set in. This prevents us from turning to God and seeking Him as our rescuer. Once we've done that, we trust Him for our breakthrough. Not just the breakthrough but transformation!

Churches needing to refinance a loan can't force the bank to lend to them. They can work and put themselves in a position where a funding event is likely, but they don't control the market, the bank's appetite for this type of risk, the economic environment, the value of real estate or the giving patterns of their members. They can and need to be good managers of the money God flows to them, but that is all they really control. God creates the resources and there is something very spiritual with how He distributes them.

I see Pastors and business owners alike frustrated by a situation or monetary need that they can't fix. Often they are stressed out about it. We've all been there. I always found a certain amount of rest and peace in something that was beyond me because I knew I couldn't fix it. When I realize I don't have the power to fix my mess, I know that it's not up to me at that point. Either God rescues me, or I won't be rescued! The part I didn't get was, God designs it that way!

Partnering with God

In the finance business we are intimately familiar with the concept of a joint venture. Two parties wishing to work together enter into a partnership. They both have vested interest in the project and work together to bring about its completion. Their goals are defined and their roles are as well. The financial partner does not look to the working manager of the business to put in capital. The working partner accepts that when he needs something financial, he will go talk to his partner, since he does not have the funds by himself. He is responsible for the operations and management of the monies invested into the company to ensure its profitable operation day-today, but even if that goes sideways, more capital may be part of a change of course.

God is a relational God. He wants to dwell with man. He walked with Adam in the cool of the day and named the animals with Him. He wants to create, partner and participate with us. If we could do it all ourselves, we wouldn't need Him. Even when we muck things up, He is still there. Even after Adam and Eve directly disobeyed God, he still provided for them. He made clothes for them. It was a mess that they couldn't fix, but it didn't change who God was. He made us to rely on Him. The thought that we can live, work, create and prosper without God is so contrary to Scripture, it's almost laughable. We weren't designed that way!

God is my Father and like a Father he has my best interest in mind. He seeks my well-being and protection and He enjoys providing for what I need. Sometimes, when I have been through a particularly difficult time, I feel abandoned, rejected, alone and forgotten. In spite of my feelings, nothing could be further from the truth. He creates men, puts a dream in our hearts, gives us the abilities to fulfill that dream and the resources we need to get the job done. He brings everything to the table and only asks for our trust and our effort. We don't accomplish His will by doing nothing, but we do it by being the one we were created to be!

Sideways

Have you ever had a track record of perceived failure where you just felt like giving up? It's very frustrating and can make one feel just about worthless. But God created us with His plan for the world in mind. He took a dream and built a person around it. He knows who we are and what we are created to be.

> *This is what the LORD says: "When seventy years are completed for Babylon, I will come to you and fulfill my good promise to bring you back to this place. For I know the plans I have for you," declares the LORD, "plans to prosper you and not to harm you, plans to give you hope and a future. Then you will call on me and come and pray to me, and I will listen to you. You will seek me and find me when you seek me with all your heart. I will be found by you," declares the LORD, "and will bring you back from captivity..."*
>
> **Jeremiah 29:11-14a (NIV)**

Our Father knows when we are in exile and need His rescue. He knows that living our lives in a way that is not what we are intended to be causes us to experience lack. We lack fulfillment, we lack resources, we lack being in our place and our destiny and the world around us lacks because we are not who we are created to be. When we lack, our piece in the world is not complete. That is why it is so vitally important to know who we are and what we were created for.

There are times in everyone's life when they forget who they are. Most of us get a little off track, sometimes way off track! The Father heart of God seeks to bring us back to that place of dependency and fulfillment in Him. When we look to other things in our lives: money, relationships, cars, houses, success or experiences to bring us happiness we get off track very quickly and our lives can become consumed by these things.

Exile is not the Promised Land. Your promised land is fulfilling who you are created to be. When we focus on the resources needed to create that vision or dream, we lose sight of our purpose. There is no lack with God. He will not call us to do something and then fail to provide the resources necessary for its accomplishment. He is the consummate partner and is faithful even when we fail.

Everything that God, our Father does is out of His love for us. When He allows challenges in our lives, it is to get our attention, to correct us, and to allow us to get back on the course that He has planned for us where there is maximum blessing and fulfillment. He equips us with all that we need so that we can be the people that He has called us to be. Sometimes this requires adjustment in our lives. One of the most common ways throughout Scripture that He does this is through money. We will see this as a thread throughout our studies of the Biblical models.

In the Bible many times when Israel, God's people, got off track, He would allow them to experience hardship. In this experiencing, they would cry out to Him, return to Him and get back on task. Although

God is the one who allows and sometimes creates these challenges, it is important to keep in mind His Father's heart. It is His extravagant love that will allow situations in our lives to bring us back to Him, back to the source of true happiness and fulfillment. Because He loves us, He won't leave us out there struggling to find peace and rest. He will seek us out and bring us back to Himself.

God rescues

Part of who He is, His innate character is a Savior, a rescuer, and a redeemer. We see this pattern over and over again in Scripture where He takes a people that are in exile, bondage and slavery and He reaches in and rescues them; sets them free. God desires us to be free, to be who we are created to be. Oftentimes, the character we need to be that person is forged through difficult experiences and challenges. Though God may allow difficulties in your life, it is very important that you know and constantly remember that His desire is to rescue you!

God resources

One of the names of God is Jehovah-Jireh, which literally means, our Provider. His will is to provide for you all the things you need. The Bible compares God to a Father and just like a Father would not ask His son or daughter to go to the store for Him and not give them money to get what He needs them to buy, so God, our Father will provide everything we need to complete the dream that He has put in our hearts. Imagine how different your mindset would be if you approached every dream, vision or idea with the knowledge that your couldn't fail and all your needs would be provided!

> *And my God will meet all your needs according to His glorious riches in Christ Jesus.*
>
> **Philippians 4:19**

As a Father that extravagantly loves us, He provides not just what we need, but even more, what we desire. Psalms says,

> *Delight yourself in the Lord and He will give you the desires of your heart;*
>
> **Psalm 37:4**

I see two meanings in this verse. One, as I delight in Him, His desires for me become my desires. In other words as I seek His will and delight in His ways, He places His desires for me in my heart. The second part is that He then fulfills the desires He put in my heart. He places His desires for me in my heart so I desire what He wants for me and then He gives it to me. As we draw closer to God in our relationships with Him, we can be confident that the very things that we desire are His will for us. Thus, we have no fear in praying for them, or seeking them, as they are a part of what we need to complete His will for us.

Is there a time in your life when God provided for you in a dramatic way? It is important as we renew our minds that we remember these moments. They become anchors of our renewed mind and belief system that will cause us to remember the faithfulness of God. These anchors will secure our hearts during times when our faith is being tested.

The Super Bowl Story

The first weekend in February of 2012, my friend Ted, a chiropractor in Indiana, invited me out for a couple of days where he could work on my back and neck and I could visit with him and his boys. It was an incredible weekend and I felt totally refreshed as God poured into me through him and his family. Saturday was a cool day where Ted, and his sons (Ted and Jacob) and I spent the afternoon on the campus of Notre Dame seeing the sights and taking in a hockey game. We stayed up late into the night talking about God and sharing stories and insights. I woke up Sunday morning at his house in Elkhart too late to head to church and felt God ask me if I wanted to go on an adventure with him. Absolutely! "Let's go to the Super Bowl." He responded. "WHAT?!?!" Was my thought. Indianapolis, where the game was being held, was only 3 hours away, so I hopped in the car and drove down, no tickets, no hookups, no advance planning at all.

I arrived after the first quarter was already over. The parking garages by the stadium were $100. Two blocks away parking was $80 and most lots were full and 10 blocks away the going rate was still $50 and most were full there as well. I asked God for a parking space. I soon found a park nearby (1.5 blocks away from the stadium) and asked the attendants there if I could park there. They were for buses only and told me they were not allowed to let anyone else in. They directed me to a park security officer sitting in his car on the park side of the complex. I approached his car, rolled my window down and asked him if there was a place I could park. "Just back your car up on the sidewalk here next to this park building and you'll be fine there." Awesome God! Parking for free!

I asked the attendants for directions to the entrance of the Super Bowl complex and they directed me to the convention center which led into the stadium area. I approached the gate with numerous x-ray machines and lots of security and asked about getting in. I have a press card from some work I did as a writer and they sent me to a conference room to ask about credentials. I arrived at the room but it was empty. A nice lady directed me to another room for credentials. They asked if I had submitted a request back in October. I had not since I only knew that morning I would be going! The ID staff was very nice but told me they couldn't help me.

Someone told me the press entrance was on the West side, so I figured I would walk over there to investigate and see what God would do. On my way, I was approached by a scalper who offered me a ticket for face value $800. "How much" I asked him.

"$800!" he replied.

"The game is half over" I told him.

"It's the SUPER BOWL!" he responded.

"How about $100?" He pretty much laughed and kept walking.

Once I got to the West entrance I explained that I had no credentials and began talking to one of the volunteers there. He said, "Let me get my supervisor." I told him it was no big deal; I figured I would just go watch the game at a nearby sports bar which would still be really cool. He got the supervisor anyway. The supervisor told me there was no way I was getting in without credentials or a ticket. "That's cool, thanks so much." I told him. As we were finishing our conversation, a couple walked right up to the supervisor and I and asked for directions to the corner of Maryland and West streets. I told them to come with me, I was heading that way and would show them where to go.

As we walked and talked I found out that the husband Vic, was a Papa John's pizza employee in North Carolina who had won a sales contest and thus won tickets for him and his wife Mandy. They told me they had had some fun. They had a guy sitting behind them that was swearing at them when Vic stood up to take a picture and Mandy had to bless this guy out in defense of her husband. Their day had been full with the experience but they were both tired and had had enough. They wanted to find their bus and head back to the hotel. I told them, I would help them and take them right to it. They asked what I was doing and I told them of my adventures of the day. They said, "Neither of the teams playing are really our teams and we're tired. If you help us find our bus, you can have one of our tickets!"

As we walked, they told me how much money they'd spent and how expensive the weekend had been for them. I was willing to offer the scalper $100 for a ticket, I thought I should at least give them something. I blessed them with $60 and they handed me the ticket - third tier balcony, right on the 50 yard line!!! Come on God! I ran back to the gate, breezed through security and into the stadium. This was so incredible! The place was electric with excitement and absolutely packed!

I found my way to my seat and settled in early 3rd quarter. I was in balcony level 3, row 2, about 3 feet off the small glass barricade and a 75 foot drop to the level below. As I walked into my seat, I leaned backwards thinking, if I fell forward, I could easily go over the glass and fall and that would not be good!

I was taking a lot of pictures on my phone and talking to those around me. When the Patriots scored, I stood up with the fans next to me and high-fived them and turned around to do the same to the guy behind me. He scoffed and said, "Sit down and take some more pictures!" Ok buddy, I thought. Then it dawned on me, might that be the guy one row back that was giving Vic and Mandy a hard time?

I texted a picture to a friend of mine who responded, "Yeah right, nice pic of the TV..." He didn't believe I was there. Of course, why would he? I had told no one except Ted and his family what I was up to that day. I stood up and turned around to take a picture of me with the field and the game in the background to prove to him I was REALLY there. I had my phone out at arms length to snap a shot when all of the sudden, the guy behind, the guy behind me fell really hard into the guy directly behind me. He hit him so hard that the guy behind me was knocked completely off his feet and out of his row, literally airborne. Since I already had my arms out and was standing up facing him, I just naturally caught him, right in my arms. I was perfectly positioned to catch this guy at the moment of his fall, it was almost as if I knew what was going to happen.

I sat him down in my chair and them helped him back up onto his feet and into his row. He was shaken up pretty good since we were so close to the balcony edge and was very grateful I broke his fall. "Oh my gosh dude (paraphrase)! Thanks so much for catching me! Oh my gosh (again paraphrase) that was intense. Thanks so much, man!"

The rest of the game passed without incident. The guy behind me and I became friends and celebrated the Giants win together. I just sat there for the trophy presentation and post-game festivities and basked in the presence and favor of God. As I got up to leave, I found a couple of Super Bowl XLVI seat cushions that apparently were on every seat and grabbed a few as souvenirs.

As I made my way back to my car, my heart was so full of how much God cared for me to bring me on this adventure! The whole weekend was awesome, but today topped my wildest expectations! On my walk to the parking lot, a Police Officer asked about the seat cushions I was carrying. "They were left in the stadium, you want one?" I asked. "Well I don't want to take one from you." He replied. "It's ok, I have four, here take one."

"Wow, thank you so much. I really appreciate it." he said. "Are you kidding me?!" I thought. My God provided me 50-yard line tickets to the SUPER BOWL!!! As I drove home, I called a bunch of people and told them the story. We laughed at how ridiculous it all sounded from waking up in the morning, driving 3 hours, seemingly, on a whim to knowing how the day ended and all that transpired in it.

Of all the fun that happened that day, God reminded me of the man who fell. The couple that left had left a two-seat wide empty space directly in front of this man leaving nothing to break his fall and possibly his plunge to his death over the balcony railing. He had perfectly positioned me to be there to catch him! WOW!

God sends

In giving us His desires for us, we see another facet of who He is. Bruce Wilkinson in his book, the *Dream Giver,* talks about how God takes a dream (purpose, destiny or vision) and builds a person around it. He gives that person all the tools they need to complete that dream. He calls us, gives us a vision, and sends us on a journey. God did that for me when I launched my finance company. He gave me the desire to do more than the residential mortgages I was doing at the time. So when I launched a commercial finance firm, I sought His ideas for a name. He gave me the name Vizion Funding. I call a vizion – a God dream. To me it's different than a vision that is man-breathed. A vizion is a calling, destiny or purpose that comes from God.

To truly understand finances and economics from a Biblical perspective it is critical to have an understanding of the Creator of money and His design for it and me. Do you know what your vizion is? Have you written it down? Do you have a plan in place to achieve it?

> *Then the Lord replied: Write the vision down and make it plain that a herald may run with it, for the vision is for the appointed time, it speaks of the end and will not prove false. Though it tarry, wait for it, it will surely come to pass and will not delay.*
>
> **Habakkuk 2:2-3**

Biblical Model – Exodus

As I struggled with this church loan in Florida, that didn't want to get done, I started searching for the model that I was to return to. At this point, I honestly questioned the relevancy of the Bible on what I do and the current state of finance in the world. I believed that the Bible was truth and had incredible wisdom for life on many levels, but I felt that things were way more complex than what God's Word addressed in this area. The first building built to house the presence of God was the tabernacle built in the desert when the Israelites left Egypt, arguably the first church. So I figured it was a good place to start.

Road to Egypt

The Israelites were in slavery in Egypt for some 400 years. They initially became enslaved when they were just a family, as a means of saving themselves from a very severe famine equivalent to a depression. Joseph, their younger brother who they had sold into slavery, went through quite a journey of his own. After being the chief servant in the household of a ruler in Egypt, he was falsely accused of attempting to seduce his master's wife, and thrown in prison. There, he found favor with the warden and was put in charge of all who were held there. Finally, after interpreting the dreams of two fellow inmates, he was remembered and brought before Pharaoh to interpret two dreams for him. (Genesis 37 – 41)

In the first dream, he was standing by the Nile, when out of the river came seven cows, sleek and fat, and they grazed among the reeds. After them, seven other cows, ugly and gaunt, came up out of the Nile and stood beside those on the riverbank. The cows that were ugly and gaunt ate up the seven sleek, fat cows. Then Pharaoh woke up.

He fell asleep again and had a second dream: Seven heads of grain, healthy and good, were growing on a single stalk. After them, seven other heads of grain sprouted—thin and scorched by the east wind. The thin heads of grain swallowed up the seven healthy, full heads. Then Pharaoh woke up.

Pharaoh's dreams were about seven years of plenty followed by seven years of famine. Joseph not only had the interpretation the dreams, but also was given a strategy for what action he should take in light of their revelations. Pharaoh saw the wisdom and favor on Joseph and placed him in charge of his entire kingdom. He appointed him to administer the saving up of the stores for the seven years of famine. As a result, Joseph stored up so much grain that it could not all be counted. The storehouses were full and so he kept the grain within the walls of the city. When the seven years of famine came, there was plenty to eat in Egypt. Everyone around came to Egypt to buy food. Joseph's brothers were no exception.

After an emotional reuniting of Joseph with his brothers and his father, Israel, Pharaoh welcomed them to Egypt and set them up as ranchers in a place called Goshen. They lived there and prospered greatly. (Genesis 41 – 50) After many years had passed, Joseph and his brothers had died and were forgotten by the new Pharaoh. The Israelites became so numerous, that the Egyptians were afraid of them and sought to control them. They oppressed them, by putting them under the rule of slave masters forcing them into slave labor. (Exodus 1:1-14)

The Exodus

Fast-forward about 400 years from when they arrived and God sends Moses to lead His people out of Egypt and free them from slavery. After ten plagues, the Egyptians were very anxious for the Israelites to leave. Moses directs them to ask their neighbors for articles of gold and silver so when they left, they plundered Egypt. (Exodus 3 – 12)

***

Historical Context

In 1446 B.C., God used Moses to free the Israelites from slavery in Egypt. Pharaoh (Amenhotep II) initially refused to let them go causing God to unleash the 10 plagues. After the final plague (the death of the firstborn), the Egyptians were very anxious for the Israelites to leave. Moses directed them to ask their neighbors for gold, silver and clothing and so, upon leaving, they plundered the richest country in the world.

***

Not only were they freed from the harsh conditions of slavery and exile, not only were they set free to find a land for themselves and become a nation, they were resourced in great abundance as they left Egypt. It is very critical to note that God didn't just grant them their freedom. He did not just have their debt forgiven and take them up to a zero balance to start over again someplace else with nothing. He resourced them in grand fashion to allow them to have all they needed for the journey and for everything that He called them to do.

Wealth of Egypt

It is also interesting to note that if you wanted to birth a nation having them incubated in an environment where they were blessed and could grow would be highly advisable. What better place than the most developed and prosperous empire of its time? Being in Egypt, they learned the latest architecture and building techniques, ways of governing, leadership, arts, craftsmanship and skilled trades. It is also conceivable that they learned philosophy, language, writing, warfare tactics and strategy, and a wide variety of other skills, trades and competencies that would put them ahead of many of the nations around them.

There was a deposit made in Egypt that provided them with the tools and education they needed for the collective call that God had on their lives both as individuals (as we see in Moses' case) and corporately as a nation.

> **There was a deposit made in Egypt that provided them with tools for their purpose.**

They did not just leave with the physical wealth of Egypt, but they also left with a wealth of education and experience that would serve them well in launching their new nation.

One thing that I see a lot working with business startups and funding at various tiers in a project or idea launch is that many times people think the number one thing they need is money. I see this over and over again. Many times business plans are not done, or certainly not done well enough to provide the road map needed for a funding event to occur. Infrastructure is often lacking. Training is still needed in many cases, legal structures set in place, entities formed, paperwork filed and recorded, teams put together, boards sat, job descriptions written, expectations in place, research done. Funding and resources in general are really only a part of what is needed to launch a dream at any level and when God is driving the plan, He will provide for all of the needs, including the things we may overlook, like character.

The Tabernacle

After departing Egypt, the dramatic deliverance from the pursuing Egyptian army at the parting of the Red Sea and several other adventures in the desert, they were led to Mount Sinai. God shares with Moses how He will dwell with man through the tabernacle. Moses receives a detailed plan, list of materials and even procedures for the administration of the tabernacle and all surrounding it. Moses shared with the nation of Israel the plans including the materials needed and how it was to be constructed.

> *"Moses said to the whole Israelite community, "This is what the LORD has commanded: From what you have, take an offering for the LORD. Everyone who is willing is to bring to the LORD an offering of gold,*

silver and bronze; blue, purple and scarlet yarn and fine linen; goat hair; ram skins dyed red and another type of durable leather; acacia wood; olive oil for the light; spices for the anointing oil and for the fragrant incense; and onyx stones and other gems to be mounted on the ephod and breastpiece."

Exodus 35:4-9

The most interesting part of this whole passage to me is how it compares to what we do today to raise money for a church building project. Every capital campaign that I have seen is based on giving pledges, which are basically promises to God and the church to pay a set amount, over and above regular giving. These funds are specifically assigned to the building fund for the purposes of monetizing the commitment from the church to the bank. These pledges are used to achieve a debt instrument (a loan or a bond) with which the church can then pay the builder, the architect and the workmen.

In this verse, Moses is very clear about what the Lord has commanded "From what you have, take an offering..." a very different approach. The idea of a pledge to build a building is the equivalent of a debt to God. It equates to putting our people in debt in order to put our churches in debt. It's a debt upon debt methodology. In the sense of building a building, particularly a house for Him or a place for Him to dwell, it's not a Biblical concept.

God took an exilic people in debt and bondage, literally slavery, and He delivered them. He set them free. It was not something they could do on their own. They were powerless for over 400 years to redeem themselves and I believe that's exactly how God wanted it. There is a great and growing movement in this country and around the world against human trafficking. When people are torn from the clutches of the lifestyle of sexual slavery, many of which are children, we call it being rescued. That is exactly what God did here. He rescued a group of people who were unable to free themselves and brought them out of the circumstance of slavery and forced labor.

But He didn't stop there. Not only did He rescue them, but He also resourced them. He provided so much more than they could have imagined upon the exodus of their enslaved condition. They had no debt, nor did they owe any one anything, no promissory notes, mortgages or credit cards. Everything they had was theirs and they had much! Being out of debt is a return to zero; out of the negative and up to a zero balance. It's freeing not to owe anyone, but it is not abundantly blessed.

So after the rescue was executed and they received willingly the plunder from their former masters, God sent them on a

> **God takes an exilic, debt-ridden people and He rescues, resources and sends them.**

journey, a mission, a grand adventure. This is a Biblical pattern that I see and it describes a facet of the character of God. He takes an exilic people, debt ridden and in bondage and He rescues them, resources them and sends them. We see it over and over again sometimes with a different twist or in a different order, but always including those three components. God rescues us, He resources us, and He sends us.

Giving to God

The freedom of giving in the method in which God commanded Moses to take up the offering for the tabernacle is incredible! He said *"From what you have, take an offering to the LORD. Everyone who is willing..."* The response was: *"Then the whole Israelite community withdrew from Moses' presence, and everyone who was willing and whose heart moved them came and brought an offering to the LORD for the work on the tent of meeting, for all its service, and for the sacred garments."*

Three components of the givers at this event were (1) they had the ability to give, (2) they were willing and (3) their hearts moved them. When I first saw this distinction, I separated two qualifications for the givers. I saw that they had the ability to give and that their hearts were moved. Being willing and having your heart moved, to me, was one and the same.

It all sounded pretty basic to me, no real revelation at all. Obviously, in order to give, you have to have something to give. Also, you heart has to be moved to give or you wouldn't give. Nothing earth-shattering here! Or so I thought...

As I read further, I came to the conclusion of the building campaign for the tabernacle. The workmen who were doing the work on the tabernacle left their work and came to Moses and told him that they had *"...more than enough to complete the work..."* and so Moses restrained the people from giving anymore. It was at this point that I literally threw my Bible down on the couch with a big, "YEAH RIGHT!" I have NEVER been to a church that has said, "Whatever you do, don't give us money." (Remember, I was frustrated...) This, of course did not help! How am I supposed to help churches when I work with multi-million dollar commercial loans and underwriting of these deals? What did all this have to do with anything?

Ability to Give

In the midst of my frustration, I felt God ask me "How do you do it?" meaning how do we raise money for building campaigns. I told Him, we spend a lot of time explaining and sharing the vision. Sometimes using a marketing company, we produce vision boards, tri-fold color brochures, heart warming, and tear jerking videos of the people our church has touched. We talk about how it's "not about the building, but about the people". We get as many people involved in the campaign as possible, having small group meetings in people's homes with the Pastor and hearing the vision both from the pulpit and in smaller settings. We have large numbers of volunteers because those who are personally vested in the campaigns have a tendency to own it and typically give more.

> **Fun Fact to Know: The gifts given to build the tabernacle have a modern-day equivalent value of over $87 Billion! That's $87,000,000,000!**

To all of this, God responded, "Hmmm, well you do part of it..." Basically, modern church culture is very good at moving the hearts of people. But if people have to have the ability to give AND have their hearts moved, then all we are doing is half. I wonder if that is why many of these campaigns are marginally effective? The question came to me, "Where did they get the ability to give?" The answer of course is that they plundered Egypt. God gave them the ability to give through His leader Moses by using him to bring the Israelites out of debt and bondage, and blessing them with great resources.

Where is that model today? How do we lead our churches into having an ability to give prior to asking them for an offering for a building? The short answer is, we don't! What if there was a campaign to free the people of a given body from the debt that they have and the financial bondage that most of us are in, prior to launching a capital campaign? I wonder what the effectiveness of a campaign done that way (the Biblical way) would be.

In this economic environment, launching a capital campaign with the financial situations most of us face (70% of Americans live paycheck to paycheck) is equivalent to taking up an offering for the tabernacle when the Israelites were still in Egypt making bricks without straw. I would imagine Moses getting a brick upside the head for even suggesting such a thing!

So how is it supposed to be? What is the model here that we can learn from and apply? I personally settled the issue somewhere along in this journey, that if it's in the Bible, there has to be a way to practically do it today. The Word of God is living and active, not only that but practical and applicable today in the most literal of senses. Much of the struggle in this journey I have been on is how do we practically implement the economic and financial blueprint in the Bible in modern society. The problem, of course, is not that it's impossible, it's just that we have been so far removed from the model or pattern, that it takes an entirely new way of thinking to get back on track. Thinking out of the box? Forget the box! Blow up the box! It can't exist on this ride!

What does all this mean to me? This was my question as I was looking for a simple solution for the challenge at hand, a way to fund the loan on the church in Florida. Perhaps Moses' greatest legacy was the deliverance of his people from debt and bondage.

Why Debt?

Debt is the system of the world and based on so many false premises, it's ridiculous! Debt started when people were using gold as a currency. Often, people would have a goldsmith hold onto their gold and even store it in their vaults for safe-keeping. It became too tedious to go and fetch the gold every time someone wanted to make a purchase and so they developed the idea of an IOU or promissory note from the goldsmith ensuring the person had that amount on deposit with him.

Soon people began trading notes instead of the gold. When the goldsmiths figured they could write more notes than they had gold and it was very unlikely that everyone at once would come and pull their gold out at the same time, debt was created. Goldsmiths did exactly that, they started writing notes for gold they didn't have in their vaults, in essence writing and IOU on an IOU. When people found out what was happening, and that there wasn't much gold in the vaults, they revolted against the goldsmiths which equated to a run on the bank.

Debt can be created out of nowhere, it happens all the time. The problem with debt is that it is an obligation that ties one financially to another person or organization, and usually has a penalty called interest that is tacked on causing the cost to go up the longer it takes to pay it off. When we don't store up and our quality of life is threatened, we use debt to buy us out, mortgaging our future.

In some cases, debt is viewed today as the standard of the day. It's how you buy a house, a car or even clothes, shoes or video games, until you get paid and have the money to pay it off. Once we're in debt, it becomes increasingly difficult to get out of it. The

> **Leading people out of debt and bondage and showing them how to have the "ability to give" is a sacred responsibility of spiritual leaders.**

worst part is we often don't turn to God to deliver us from our bondage.

Debt and Grace

Many view debt as OUR problem. We created it and we just need to pay it. We believe God can save the alcoholic and the drug addict. He can deliver them and set them free from bondages caused by their own actions. Yet when we've made poor financials choices, over spent on our credit cards and mortgaged our futures, we think we have to fight and earn our way out. That's not grace, it's not the Biblical model and it's certainly not the heart of God. Remember the model we see in the Word is that God rescues us, resources us and sends us on a mission, a calling or a destiny.

We didn't deserve salvation either. In fact the strict standards of the law were to show people their need for a Savior. We can't be righteous on our own, what makes us think we can earn our way to financial freedom? The Israelites knew that their only hope for freedom was divine action by God. That's a good description of many of our financial situations today. It doesn't mean we stay in the same pattern. We need to take responsibility and change our behavior. It does mean we need a deliverer to lead us out.

After leading the Israelites out of Egypt, Moses received the orders from God to build the tabernacle and took up an offering. ***Those who had the ability to give, whose hearts moved them, and who were willing, gave.*** Sounds simple, right? But where did they get the "ability to give"? From God, through Moses, in perhaps the most divinely inspired act of his life.

Economic Strategy First Revealed

As I researched this further, I began to wonder when God planned the strategy of rescuing the Israelites AND providing them with resources to have the ability to give to the tabernacle building project. We see just before they leave, they did what Moses told them to do; they ask the Egyptians for articles of silver, gold and for clothing in Exodus 12:36. So, my question was, when did God tell Moses? In Exodus 11:2, God outlined the instructions for Moses to tell the people to plunder Egypt.

I felt, for some reason that that was not the end of the matter. I found that at the burning bush when God called Moses to leave Midian, return to Egypt and free His people, that He gave them the same instructions

(Exodus 3:21-22). Also, it is interesting to note that in verse 8 when He was telling Moses who He was, He said that

> *...I have indeed seen the misery of my people in Egypt. I have heard them crying out because of their slave drivers, and I am concerned about their suffering. So I have come down to rescue them from the hand of the Egyptians and to bring them up out of that land into a good and spacious land, a land flowing with milk and honey.*
>
> **Exodus 3:7-8**

For some reason, again the matter was not settled with me. I was guided to God's covenant with Abraham, where God told him,

> *Know for certain that for four hundred years your descendants will be strangers in a country not their own and that they will be enslaved and mistreated there. But I will punish the nation they serve as slaves, and afterward they will come out with great possessions.*
>
> **Genesis 15:13-14**

This was incredible, an absolute epiphany for me! You mean God had a financial plan for the children of Israel some 500+ years before it ever happened?!?! This discovery was totally a revelation to me in the fact that God not only cares about finances and economics but that He had a plan, literally hundreds of years in advance of their happening that includes every detail of how He will bless His people and provide a great abundance and increase that will allow them to partner with Him in building the physical structure in which He will dwell with man. AWESOME!

The other part of this revelation, that I only saw recently, was the fact that He gave people the blessing first, without requiring a return. He didn't command that all the people give the plunder of Egypt to the building project. He didn't use any form of stick or carrot or any kind of manipulation in any form. What He did do was to bless His people, rescue them, resource them and then invite them into a partnership opportunity, totally of their own free will to be a part of creating a structure where He would dwell with man: a house for Himself on earth that He would fill with His Glory and occupy.

It's not as if God needs us to build Him a house. He doesn't need anything from us. He certainly doesn't need gifts or offerings from us to provide for His housing. The earth is the Lord's and everything in it! But they were given the opportunity to partner with Him, to have a role, a part, to create the very house that His Glory would fill. In the verses in Exodus 35 and 36 describing the capital campaign, if you will, it mentions the words, "those willing" 7 times and "freewill offering" twice. It seems to be a point that God wanted emphasized in this model. It was expressed a total of 9 times that there was not an obligation to give, to partner with God, but those willing could do so.

God allowed the Israelites to be in Egypt; in fact He used Egypt to save them from certain death when there was a severe famine. The Israelites were living as slaves in Egypt. God used Moses to free them from bondage, debt and slavery. He then resourced them with more than they had ever had before and sent them on a mission, or better said, invited them into an adventure with Him – to build a tabernacle where He would dwell with us. God not only invites us into partnership with Him, He rescues us from debt and bondage and provides us with the resources so that we can!

The results speak for themselves. In a short amount of time, they had more than enough to complete the work and had to be restrained from giving anymore. I find the use of the word "restrained" from giving interesting. It's as if the time for partnering with God on this project had a lifespan, a time frame. At some point the opportunity had passed.

Biblical Model – Haggai

The redemptive power of God, His grace and favor demonstrated through freedom and finance is twice illustrated in the story surrounding the rebuilding of the temple in Jerusalem detailed in Ezra and Haggai. The Jews were in exile in Babylon when God sends Cyrus, the Persian King to conquer Babylon and give favor to His people. King Cyrus released 50,000 Jews and sent them back to Jerusalem. (Ezra 1:1-8) Before leaving, they took an offering from their friends and neighbors, like they did in Egypt, to fund their trip. (Ezra 1:6, 2:68-69) They were rescued, resourced and sent.

Once back in Jerusalem they started rebuilding the Temple as God and King Cyrus had directed them. They worked for two years and in the face of strong opposition, they stopped. They instead built their own houses. God caused an economic recession (drought & famine) to get their attention. This is a Biblical example of how God allows or causes, recession to get the attention of His people because they got off-course. (Haggai 1)

***

Historical Context

In 538 B.C., the conqueror of Babylon, Cyrus king of Persia, issued a decree allowing the Jews to return to Jerusalem and rebuild the temple. About 50,000 Jews journeyed home and began to work on the temple. They laid the foundations, which took them 2 years and they stopped. God spoke through Haggai the prophet to Zerubbabel the Governor of Judah and Joshua, the high priest.

***

The Lord Almighty confronts His people on the issue of their disobedience in completing the task of rebuilding the temple. The people had stopped the building project but had built their own *paneled* houses instead.   "Paneled houses" refers to the opulent homes constructed of cedar paneling usually connected with houses of royalty. He asks them if it's time for them to live in their paneled houses while His house remains a ruin. Because of their failure to complete their calling, God caused the heavens to withhold their dew and the earth it's crops resulting in a drought and famine.

> *Now this is what the LORD Almighty says: "Give careful thought to your ways. You have planted much, but harvested little. You eat, but never have enough. You drink, but never have your fill. You put on clothes, but are not warm. You earn wages, only to put them in a purse with holes in it. This is what the LORD Almighty says: "Give careful thought to your ways. Go up into the mountains and bring down timber and build my house, so that I may take pleasure in it and be honored," says the LORD. "You expected much, but see, it turned out to be little. What you brought home, I blew away. Why?"*

declares the LORD Almighty "Because of my house, which remains a ruin, while each of you is busy with your own house. Therefore, because of you the heavens have withheld their dew and the earth its crops. I called for a drought on the fields and the mountains, on the grain, the new wine, the olive oil and everything else the ground produces, on people and livestock, and on all the labor of your hands."

Haggai 1:5-11

God-owned Recession

The Lord Almighty described to Israel the economic recession that they are feeling. This is the most incredible description of not only what recession is, but also how it feels. "What you brought in, I blew away..." It feels like a no-win scenario! Frankly, that's exactly what it's designed to be, especially in this case. God takes ownership for causing the recession and then tells them exactly why it's happening.

There are numerous other instances in the Bible when recession occurs, but for this passage alone, every single time there is a recession whether personally or globally, we should give careful thought to our ways. I do not believe recession to be judgment from God. Jesus took all of our sin and the curse and penalty for it on the cross. I do believe it is a tool of alignment.

God, our Father, loves us dearly. He wants to pour into us everything we need and desire, but many times, without the proper alignment, it would kill us. Without our attention on Him and the purpose for which

He has called us, an abundance of wealth can literally be a curse. Jesus Himself said, "How hard it is for a rich man to enter the Kingdom of heaven." Again, it goes back to relationship. God wants us to look to Him as our rescuer, giver of resource, and sender, but more than that, as a Father who does all those things out of His extravagant love for us.

Careful Thought...

God encourages them to give careful thought to their ways and to get back to work. Remember, they were in exile in Babylon when this whole thing started. He rescued them, resourced them and sent them back to Jerusalem with abundance to complete the task of rebuilding His temple. He had one king conquer another and then moved that Gentile king's heart to want him to build a temple to the God of heaven. Is it possible that after all this, they forgot why they were sent back? That is why God encourages them to give careful thought to their ways. They knew the history.

Because of God's words to the people through His prophet Haggai, the people repent, come together in unity and obedience and renew their work on the temple. Three months later, the Lord Almighty says that *"from this day forward"* I will bless you. He restores the financial blessing and the recession is over. (Haggai 2:10-19) It's incredible to realize that God's people and their actions ended the recession! This second time, He sends them to do the work first, then He rescues them from the famine and resources them by restoring the abundance.

What does this mean to me?

When God tells the inhabitants of
Jerusalem about their recession, He
makes it a point to say, *"because of you,
the heaven's have withheld their dew and*

> **It's incredible to realize that God's people and their actions ended the recession!**

the earth its crops..." That is not a regional problem! It is amazing the
repercussions that the actions of God's people have on the world. We
set the tone! One of the main reasons Biblically for recessions, even
large scale ones, is to get the attention and thus the proper alignment of
His people. And so today, as we experience global recession, should we
not give careful thought to our ways?

I believe that the economic recession we are experiencing right now is
the same. God desires to get the attention of His people so we can make
some much needed changes in our personal lives, financial lives,
priorities and ministry models. We have been heading down some
roads and working with methods that will simply not get the job done.
Without getting our attention and challenging us in a major way, we will
likely persist in flawed systems and mentalities like the Israelites did in
Haggai.

So what grand assignment are we called to do that we are not doing?

> *Then Jesus came to them and said, "All authority in
> heaven and on earth has been given to me.
> Therefore go and make disciples of all nations,
> baptizing them in the name of the Father and of the
> Son and of the Holy Spirit, and teaching them to obey*

everything I have commanded you. And surely I am
with you always, to the very end of the age."

Matthew 28:18-20

Are there other parallels with the book of Haggai and the church today? I think so. Their mandate was to come together, in unity and build the temple. What is the temple today? Jesus, during His ministry, told the Pharisees,

"Destroy this temple, and I will raise it again in three days."

John 2:19

What Temple?

We know that He was not referring to the physical structure of the temple in Jerusalem, but His body. So what is the body of Christ in the earth today? It's US! It is the church or the *ecclesia*, which literally means "the called out ones". So if the collective church, the body of Christ, in the earth today is what we are called to build, is that not the vizion laid out in the Great Commission? By making disciples of all nations, we are building the body of Christ in the earth today.

We need a massive effort on a global scale to accomplish this momentous task. No one can be left out. Everyone has a piece, a place on the wall. In the age of the computer, concord jets, satellites and renewable energy, how come the whole world has not heard the Gospel? Why are there still some 639 unengaged, unreached people groups of over 150,000 in population that have not heard? Some would say that it's a lack of resources. Could it be a lack of unity and focus?

Paneled Houses?

What are the "paneled houses"? Could these be the kingdoms we create in our own lives, churches and individual ministries as we seek to build them outside of the corporate vision and unity in the body of Christ today? Many churches in America have vast opulent houses, some with $100M price tags or more. I am not against big churches, make no mistake, but are we working together in unity to build the body of Christ in the earth? Are we working together in a coordinated strategy towards the call of God on our collective lives – the Great Commission? If not, is it not demonstrated here with Biblical precedence that God would allow a global financial shaking equivalent to the recession in Haggai to get our attention and refocus us?

This is a word, not just for churches either but for individuals as well. Finding your vizion, your piece in the Great Commission is doing your part to build the temple. The choice is yours. Do you know what your vizion is? Do you have it written down plainly? If not, you are missing the most important piece of your entire life. It's what your life is all about. Without it, you have no direction or purpose. Finances won't cure a life without purpose. Finding your vizion is the very first step in the journey.

But I don't know my calling - *so find out!* Take time to seek the Lord, get in His presence and ask Him what your calling is. Bring a notebook along and write down your thoughts, don't filter! Ask a couple of key questions: What am I passionate about? What are my talents and skills? What can I do to be part of fulfilling the Great Commission? Once you feel you have it, test it, pray some more, talk to Godly counsel and then begin moving in that direction by setting goals. You will embark on the most incredible adventure of your life!

***

One more revival; only one more is needed; the revival of Christian stewardship; the consecration of the money power of the Church unto God and when that revival comes the Kingdom of God will come in a day. You can no more prevent it than you can hold back the tides of the ocean.

Horace Bushnell (1902)

***

I love this quote from Horace Bushnell, which first appeared in a Christian magazine in 1902. To me it says it all. The way we handle money has prevented us from fulfilling our vizions and has kept the world from hearing the redemptive message of the Gospel. The good news is, if we turn this one thing around, I believe like Horace, that the Kingdom of God will come in a day and nothing can prevent it! Do you personally take ownership of the Great Commission? How does your vizion fit into the Great Commission? What are you doing about it?

Biblical Model - Nehemiah

The loan for the church in south Florida that had been so difficult, eventually closed and funded some 6 months after I started on it. It was one of the longest battles to get a deal done that I had had to date. The conversations I had with God during that time launched me on a quest to understand what the Biblical models of finance and economics were. As I pray, God sometimes drops one word in my spirit and provide revelation on just one concept or facet of the economic picture. Other times He drops several.

There was a period of about 20 days, where I was directed to read Nehemiah 1-7. Everyday it was the same thing, read it again. This wasn't about building a temple, church or tabernacle, but it was a massive building project that has a lot of relevance.

Summary

Nehemiah was one of the exiles in Babylon. His job, as cupbearer to the king, was to bring the king his drink every day. When he heard news about the condition of the city of Jerusalem, that its walls were torn down and burned, he was cut to the heart. After prayer and fasting, he took action by letting the king see him sad, something that could have gotten him fired or even killed.
When the king asked what was bothering him, Nehemiah explained to him all about the city of Jerusalem and its condition. God gave him favor with the king, who then sent him back to Jerusalem to fulfill the

vision of rebuilding its wall. (Nehemiah 1, 2)

***

Historical Context

In 444 B.C., Nehemiah approached the king of Babylon, King
Artaxerxes about Jerusalem and its walls. This was four months
after he first heard the news. He took the time to fast & pray and
developed a strategy and a list of needed supplies. When the
king granted him favor, he asked for very specific things
including letters allowing him rights of passage, access to lumber
and even a military escort back to his homeland.

***

Nehemiah had an extensive plan. He asked for and was given letters of
passage to the Governors of the Trans-Euphrates and a letter to the
keeper of the king's forest to obtain lumber needed for the work. The
king also sent army officers and cavalry with him as escorts on the
journey, which was more than he asked for. Can you say favor? Once
in Jerusalem, he surveyed the damage, talked to the people and began
the work. The people worked together in unity each taking their place
on the wall to rebuild it. (Nehemiah 2 - 7)

Digging Deeper

As I read Nehemiah some 20+ times, I found myself feeling like I had a
solid grasp on the material and the message. I would ask God in my
quiet time what to study and kept hearing "read Nehemiah 1-7." After
about two and a half weeks of this, I was telling God, "I think I got it."

"Nope, read it again." he replied, and the same thing the next day. Finally, I was telling Him, "God, I got it, I really got it." I felt a challenge in the form of a question in response. "Ok, what does the wall do?"

> ### Purposes of the Wall
> **Protection** – from invaders
> **Boundary** – of city limits
> **Structure** – buildings built in the walls
> **Flow** – gates control flow in and out
> **Accountability** – a place for the watchman to stand
> **Monument** – Place of remembrance

The wall around a city in ancient times had multiple functions. It provided protection from invading armies; and safety and security for the people that lived inside the city. The city walls also marked the boundary of the city. It was very easy to tell whether you were in the city or outside of it. The lines were clear. The wall provided structure to the city itself. Buildings and even homes were built into the walls providing infrastructure to the city. Each city had several gates used to control the flow of traffic in and out. Some gates were meant for merchants, others for animals.

One of the most significant uses of the wall was as a guard tower. It's where the watchmen stood. They could see who was coming off in the distance and monitor traffic flow through the gates. This was a very important part of the security and well being of its inhabitants. The wall was a major part of the first impression of the city, the curb appeal if you will. It served as a monument or a place of remembrance. As we pride ourselves on our skylines today, the wall was the image people had of a city and was indicative of its strength and opulence.

So after listing these answers out: protection, boundaries, structure, flow, monument and a place for the watchmen to stand, I felt God ask me, "What does a financial system do for a person, a church or a country?" The answer was the same. It provides protection for those involved in it and from those who would steal or embezzle. It provides boundaries, how much can be spent and when. It provides structure or a plan. It also provides for cash flow in and out, it provides accountability or a place for the watchman to stand and it serves as a monument, or a remembrance of how we spent our lives and resources. Our walls, just like the wall of Jerusalem, need to be rebuilt!

A financial strategy is very much like an ancient city wall. A good financial strategy is more than just a financial plan. It's a way of managing your money that will give its users boundaries and structure. When constructed and maintained properly it will provide protection from would-be embezzlers and thieves. Those involved in the system will know the limits and how decisions are made. Vizion will be built into it. Budgets will provide the structured flow of cash in and out like the gates of a city. A critical function of a financial strategy is to provide the accountability ensuring the strength and well being of those involved.

Rebuilding

There is so much in the book of Nehemiah that we can learn about vizion and finances. There are many groups of people mentioned that are working on the wall. Rulers, priests, goldsmiths, perfume makers, sons, daughters, farmers, vineyard keepers, noblemen and others. Some of these groups had very specific assignments on the wall: to build this gate here or that section there. Several of the groups, the Bible says, "...*built the section directly in front of their house*..." (Nehemiah 3) What is directly in front of you is what you see or your vision (vizion). Some are called to travel to distant lands and be missionaries, some are called to travel to LA and be actors. Others are called to build their vizion right where they are, what is directly in front of them. Everyone has a piece and no part is greater than any other. Without all of the people working together, the wall will not be completed, but as we all work on our part, it will come together.

Recession & Mortgage Crisis

When a conquering army would occupy a region, it was common practice to exile the most talented people of the defeated country to live and work as slaves in the foreign power's homeland. Many of the wealthy, the business owners, those of political acumen or importance were taken from their lands to serve their new master. Those left behind were many times the poorer members of society and also those in menial positions such as farmers and ranchers. They would continue to operate in their homeland while paying hefty taxes or homage to the conquering king.

It is not surprising then that the people left in Jerusalem were experiencing economic hardship. As the project progressed, the people of Jerusalem came to Nehemiah and told him of their financial woes. It says that they "*...raised a cry of protest against their fellow Jews.*" (Exodus 5:1 (NLT)) There are three groups of Jews that beseeched Nehemiah as their leader for answers to their financial challenges. One group had large families and they needed grain to feed them. Another group mortgaged their homes, fields and vineyards to buy food during the famine. Still others owed the king taxes and had to borrow money to pay them and were forced to subject their children to slavery. The strategy that God gave Nehemiah in response to the cry of the people regarding their debt is timeless.

It's interesting to note here that in the midst of their recession (famine) there is also a mortgage crisis. Sound familiar? God has Nehemiah address the issue of debts by first canceling mortgage interest and then canceling the mortgage debt. He addresses the issue of the high interest they were paying. The Israelites were commanded by God to lend to a

> **It's interesting to note that in the midst of a recession (famine) there is a mortgage crisis. Sound familiar?**

brother in need at zero percent interest. The nobles (who were the money lenders) were charging 1% interest (the hundredth part). God called it usury. He dealt with the nobles until they agreed to cancel the debts and return all lands to their rightful owners and to give back the interest they had charged. With their debts canceled and their families fed, the people went back to work on the wall. They completed building the wall around the entire city in just 52 days! Can you imagine? Debt-free people make the best volunteers because they have **the ability to give more** of their time towards a project.

In the chapter on Grace we saw how the heart of the Father is to pull a debt-ridden, exilic people out of debt and bondage, resource them and send them on a vizion. I believe, in this story, the very reason that God sent Nehemiah back to Jerusalem to rebuild the wall was so that, in rebuilding, He would set the people free from the debt that they were in. The vizion drove the freedom in this case. He sent them on a mission first and then had to deal with the issues of debt and recession around them to empower them to complete the very task He called them to. First He rescued, resourced and sent Nehemiah. Then He sent the Jews, rescued and resourced them.

What does this mean to me?

Whether He sets us free from debt, resources us and send us on a vizion or sends us on the vizion first and in obedience to that vizion, frees us and resources us, it does not matter. The basic premise is the same – you can't lose with obedience! A key part of this is to understand that you have

> **Whether He sets us free from debt, resources us and send us on a vizion or sends us on the vizion first and in obedience to that vizion, frees us and resources us, it does not matter.**

a vizion, a calling and begin to pursue it. You have something to build right in front of you that God has called you to do. He will provide for your freedom and financial ability to make it happen. Know your vizion and get in obedience to it because God resources where He calls!

What is right in front of you that you see needs rebuilding? Has God freed you from debt and bondage, resourced you and sent you on a vizion, or has He sent you on a vizion first seemingly without resources? Where are you and what is your response to Him?

We can use the strategy that God gave Nehemiah as a divinely inspired pattern/model on how to get free from debt and bondage so that we may fulfill that calling on our lives – our vizion. By canceling mortgage (or debt) interest and mortgage (or debt) principal, we can free ourselves rapidly allowing us to focus our time, energy and resources on the vizion instead of the financial issues that have plagued us and kept us from the will of God for our lives.

What would you do more of if you were debt-free? What could a group of Christ-followers accomplish if they were debt-free and resourced with plenty of time?

Biblical Model – Joel

Haggai was a great example of how God used recession to get the attention of His people. They were given freedom, abundance and a purpose. When they failed to complete their assignment, God withheld resources (dew and crops) causing an economic recession, which resulted in their repentance and renewed obedience and thus the task was finished. Joel is different in a multitude of ways.

Historical Context

With no references to datable historic events, the book, historians believe, was penned between the late 7th and early 5th centuries B.C. The complete and sudden destruction of the economic base is followed by a massive call for unified repentance, mourning and prayer. After the people are unified and have opened their hearts to God, He answers them rescuing them from the calamity and providing resources for what lay ahead.

***

Beyond Recession

The book begins with the word of the Lord speaking to the people through the prophet describing events that had already taken place. The description begins with a call to remember if anything like this has ever happened, emphasizing the severity of the occurrence. What we find out as the account continues is that four plagues of locusts have invaded the land destroying all plant life. What each preceding plague left, the next plague ate. There is reason to believe that the first plague ate the leaves, the second the branch, the third devoured the stalk and the fourth the root, leaving nothing behind.

The resulting condition of the land is summarized as follows:

> *The fields are ruined, the ground is dried up; the grain is destroyed, the new wine is dried up, the olive oil fails. Despair, you farmers, wail, you vine growers, grieve for the wheat and the barley, because the harvest of the field is destroyed. The vine is dried up and the fig tree is withered; the pomegranate, the palm and the apple tree— all the trees of the field— are dried up. Surely the people's joy is withered away.*

Joel 1:10-12

The grain, new wine and oil, the staples of the agrarian society of its time are mentioned here as being demolished. Much like in Haggai, a withholding of these key commodities causes significant erosion of the economy. In this case though, we are talking about a sudden, complete and utter devastation.

In Haggai, Exodus and Nehemiah, there are accurate historical references that date the events told there. Joel is different in that historians have no accurate date of when Joel occurred or even if it has. The reference in verse 15, to "that day" and the "day of the Lord" again are reasons to support the premise that the account is about some time in the future near the day of the Lord and perhaps even "end-times prophetic".

> *Alas for that day! For the day of the Lord is near; it will come like destruction from the Almighty.*
>
> **Joel 1:15**

Additionally, there is the difference of the severity of the famine. What is described here would be more accurately described as a depression and a very severe one! The four plagues of locusts wipe out virtually all plant life making economic sustainability for an agrarian society impossible. The complete destruction of the economic base is not a dip in production like we see in a drought or the gradual drainage of resource stores we see in a famine. This is an all out cataclysmic devastation of the economic base. Equated throughout the account to the irreversible damage of a massive fire, there is no recovery, short of the hand of God, from this event.

The complete destruction of the economic base is not a dip in production like we see in a drought or the gradual drainage of resource stores we see in a famine.

Rend Your Hearts

The account contains no reference to exile or bondage, which is another distinction from the models we see in the other three case studies. There is no description of the sin or wrongdoing on behalf of the people that precluded these happenings. There is the call for repentance; for mourning, wailing, fasting and a crying out to the Lord. Calls to repentance were typical throughout the Old Testament during times of calamity. Many times, God revealed the reason for the calamity by means of the prophets. Again, there is not such a description here, just a call to return to the Lord.

The call for repentance and unity is more of a cleansing of the hearts of all in the land. Joel calls on everyone to repent; drunkards, farmers, vine growers, elders, children, the people, the assembly, those nursing, the bridegroom, the bride, priest and ministers. It is a consecration, a dedication of their hearts to God. Everyone in all positions, age groups, social classes and gender in society are included. The call to "rend their hearts" is extremely urgent due to the suddenness and severity of the events. There is no time to waste!

Restoration (Rescued & Resourced)

In all of this, even though it is not initially clear in the written account, there is massive purpose. God has a plan that He reveals to them in His answer. First, He promises them that He will send them *"grain, new wine, and oil, enough to satisfy you fully."* He miraculously restores the economic base. He also drives the armies out of the land, restores the pastures, the trees, and the vines. He gives them abundant showers, both autumn and spring rains, fills their threshing floors with grain and overflows their vats with new wine and oil. And then He repays them,

> *I will repay you for the years the locusts have eaten—*
> *the great locust and the young locust, the other*
> *locusts and the locust swarm— my great army that I*
> *sent among you.*
>
> **Joel 2:25**

The part about this verse that I love is the fact that God takes ownership of the destruction that just occurred. There is no doubt that He sent the locusts to align the hearts of the people and unify them in consecration before Him. He further promises them that they will never again be shamed. And then He reveals His purpose:

> *And afterward, I will pour out my Spirit on all*
> *people. Your sons and daughters will prophesy, your*
> *old men will dream dreams, your young men will see*
> *visions. Even on my servants, both men and women,*
> *I will pour out my Spirit in those days.*
>
> **Joel 2:28-29**

I have heard many people teach on the above verses. They all seem to start at the "And afterward..." part. What comes before the "and afterward" though is critical. There is a massively historic economic event in the form of a debilitating depression, followed by a call to repentance and a corporate return to God, followed by another large scale economic miracle recovery, where God restores the resources and then the outpouring. I hear teachers use this verse and the rest of Joel in describing the end times' harvest or what some call the final outpouring. I find it interesting that there is first an alignment of the hearts of the people related to their economy and resources. God is clearly using the depression to ensure their character and consecration prior to releasing the great abundance that will be needed to handle the outpouring and subsequent harvest.

God aligns them through the attack of locusts and the destruction of their economic base so they have no hope except in Him. They come together in unity, aligning their hearts, and He restores and provides an outpouring of economic abundance. Then, with His people abundantly blessed to handle the harvest and the outpouring, He pours out His Spirit on them! Once again, they are rescued, resourced and sent!

Taking Action

...humbly accept the word planted in you, which can save you. Do not merely listen to the word, and so deceive yourselves. Do what it says.

James 1:20-22

Real transformation will ultimately express itself in the way we live. Though it begins in the renewing of the mind, it is outwardly expressed through our words, our actions and finally our lifestyle. It becomes who we are. To know the Word is not enough, we must allow it to change us. To change us, we must take action.

Repentance

The Greek word for repentance, metanoia, simply means *changing of minds* or *going a different direction*. It literally means to turn around, or to change one's mind; to think and live differently. It is a main component of transformation. This journey that I have been on for the last four years has had many moments of this—realizing that there is a comprehensive economic model that is God-breathed and flawless was one of those moments. Understanding that God often speaks to His people through recession is another. Gaining a true revelation of what it means to renew my mind and transform my life were other moments and the process is still ongoing.

Change often happens in degrees; we don't necessarily turn a corner all at once. It takes a half a mile or more, depending on speed and sea conditions, to turn an aircraft carrier 90 degrees. You can't just turn right, it happens in degrees. In the same way, change occurs in people at varying rates depending on the conditions they are experiencing, how bad they want change and how much pressure is being applied to a particular part of their life. The concepts of grace in finances, and learning more about God as one who rescues, resources and sends us, were all built on the foundation of what I found in His word and seeing His provision in my own life over and over again.

> **Repentance means to turn around, or to change one's mind, to think and live differently.**

Several common themes appeared in the Biblical models as I studied them. Haggai and Joel were big on repentance as part of the process to come out of their recessions. In Nehemiah, repentance took place on the part of the leaders (nobles and officials) by forgiving the debts of the people. Repentance occurred in the mindsets of the whole nation of Israel in the Exodus account for them to leave and plunder Egypt. For the rebuilding of the wall in Nehemiah, God brought back a leader from exile to empower the people to change their minds. They began to work together to literally dig out of the rubble and rebuild with the pieces that had been there all along.

What rubble lies around us that need rebuilding? I see in my work with both churches and ministries that many are struggling. Most ministry models have a donor base supporting them, and that is struggling as well. Giving seems to be down in most areas and cutbacks have been necessary from staff at churches, to missionaries returning from the field due to lack of support. We are seeing changes in the mission models, but we also need sweeping changes in the ministry financial models to solve these challenges.

Kindness Leads

I am encouraged in this fact: God has a financial plan and He is shaking things, which means new alignments and strategies are being released for an abundant provision, like we saw in Haggai and Joel. Remember that when they were in the worst economic devastation in Joel, they were only two steps away from an abundant outpouring of both blessing and resources, and the Spirit of God!

> *Or do you think lightly of the riches of His kindness and tolerance and patience, not knowing that the kindness of God leads you to repentance?*
>
> **Romans 2:4**

His kindness leads us to repentance and with repentance comes the changing (renewing) of our minds which causes transformation. The riches of His kindness, His tolerance and patience with us and His grace, empowering favor, are intended to lead us into greater blessing and abundant provision.

So let's bring this down to the personal level. What is God adjusting or aligning in your life to bring abundant provision. Where is His kindness leading you?

Do you own the Great Commission personally? Have you determined what His vizion for your life is and how it fits into the work of making disciples of all nations? Most of us need change in our personal financial lives. We need to be serious about our vizion. If we weren't already positioned or willing to be positioned to do what we have been called to do, then why would God fund us?

Much at Stake

The number one reason why marriages fail is arguments or issues over money. If we don't get this right, so much more than just our financial lives is at stake. This is about the family! Money troubles and the mismanagement of money have been used for centuries as a tool of attack on the family. If the enemy can take out our families, he can wreak immense havoc in our lives and cause terrible pain and distraction from the real war. Money has always been a good distraction. The enemy knows it and so does God. Money is also a tool, a very powerful tool that funds vizion. It feeds the family, builds schools and churches, funds businesses and allows us to send people around the world. It is essential in every area of ministry on every part of the planet and vital for making disciples of nations. What country could exist

> **The number one reason why marriages fail is arguments or issues over money. If we don't get this right, so much more than just our financial lives is at stake!**

without money? What ministry? Our very ability to fulfill the Great Commission is dependent upon our ability to manage money correctly and to use it well, beginning on a personal level and extending to the corporate.

In Haggai, after the Lord Almighty brought to their attention why they were experiencing recession, He then simply told them to, "***Be strong and do the work.***" They had a choice to make. They needed to repent. They could continue struggling in a place of lack or they could turn around and do what God called them to do. (Haggai 2:4-5) Repentance again simply means to turn around, change one's mind, to think and live differently.

Part of the repentance or "mind change" that the body of Christ needs in this area is contained in the message of grace. We saw in all the Biblical models how God rescues, resources and sends. Knowing that we did not call ourselves and are not in this calling alone, we should not expect to fund ourselves either. Trust and reliance on God is part of the new way of thinking we need to adopt, even when we've screwed up, and even when we made the mistakes that landed us in exile.

Practicality

So how do we do this practically? There are several ways: 1) change how we think, and recognize God as the provider of all of our resources. 2) If we are in a financial mess, bring it all before Him and ask for His grace and mercy. He wants to rescue us. Remember, it's part of His nature! 3) Seek the Lord for His help in our financial lives and begin moving forward in faith and obedience. This obedience is not just to manage our lives and resources correctly, but also is obedience to the Great Commission and our vizion or calling.

Whether you're a pastor of a church, a missionary, a businessman or a stay-at-home mom, if you get on task with your calling, He will be with you and will bless you. This concept is included right in the Great Commission when He says, "*...Go...and I will be with you always...*" In Haggai 2, after the Israelites renewed their commitment to the work of the temple, God spoke to them and told them,

> *"From this day on, I will bless you."*
>
> **Haggai 2:19**

The same thing happened in Joel. Once the people repented and turned back to God, He blessed them abundantly! (Joel 2:18-27) God wants to bless us. He wants to provide for us. We need to get on task with what He called us to do. The first thing that He called us all to do is to actively participate in the Great Commission.

Impact

It's interesting to note that the onus for the lifting or removing of the destructive force from a land is on God's people. We have the authority and power. He gave it to us in Joshua 1:3, 2 Chronicles 7:14 and many other places and yet we forgot, became complacent, or attempted to turn the position over to others. The responsibility is still ours, and the Lord wants it that way. Let us not forget the words that He spoke in the hearing of Solomon as a response to his prayer upon the occasion of dedicating the temple in Jerusalem:

I have heard your prayer and have chosen this place
for myself as a temple for sacrifices. When I shut up
the heavens so that there is no rain, or command the
locusts to devour the land or send a plague among
my people, if my people, who are called by my name,
will humble themselves and pray and seek my face
and turn from their wicked ways, then will I hear
from heaven and will forgive their sin and will heal
their land.

2 Chronicles 7:12-14

"IF MY PEOPLE" should be screamed from the rooftops everywhere. If we really understood the authority that the Lord Almighty has given us, it would move us to action and repentance. What if the very thing that the Lord was looking for to remove the blight of recession and unemployment from our lands, was a call to repentance by His church? That IS what's required! If we really believed this, we wouldn't be talking about a recession anymore. It would be over! We, His people, hold the keys to the deliverance of our families, nations and the world!

Faith

Faith is the substance of things hoped for, the
evidence of things not seen.

Hebrews 11:1

Have you ever felt like you've been struggling and trying to get somewhere and no matter what you do nothing is going to work? You've struggled, sometimes for years? You've cried and prayed and sought help, but nothing. You feel alone, abandoned, rejected and useless. Feeling that way can be overwhelming and life is difficult to navigate during those time and yet, it's not true! None of it! You are not alone, you have not been abandoned, you are not rejected and you are not useless. The truth is you are extravagantly loved, cared for, thought of, remembered, accepted and valued beyond measure! It's during those times that we need to remember the Father heart of God and look back at the Biblical models to find out what we need to do.

Seeing God as our rescuer; who desires to save us, resource us and fulfill a dream in His heart and ours by sending us on our purpose, is part of the mind change many of us need. The God of the whole universe is the one who called you, commissioned you, pursued you when you were not looking for Him and who died to cover all of your sin before any of it was even committed. Do you think that He would allow a lack of any resource to stop you from achieving the very thing that He has called you to do? Having that faith, that knowledge of who He is, the patterns that we see above and the simple acceptance of His grace and favor in our lives, will change everything! You will find yourself calm in the storms, dancing through

> **Do you think the God of the universe who called you would allow a lack of resources to stop you from achieving the very thing He called you to do?**

them. You will be happy in the midst of challenges, and you will have the confidence to radically and wholeheartedly commit to your vizion even when you have no clue how it will happen.

With faith, the strong conviction and belief that God has a plan for your life and He is in control, we have hope, and with hope, the Gospel has meaning. Gospel simply means "good news". With faith in the provision of our Father and His grace and favor on our lives, we have hope. Without hope, there is no good news!

Faith and Intimacy

The promises of God are all throughout Scripture. When we truly understand the heart of the Father, and know Him relationally, we know that we don't need to worry about money, ever! He has everything we need and He is more than able to supply abundantly more than we can ask or think. Our job is not to worry, but to focus on Him and what He's called us to do. He will provide. We are actually commanded to not worry and to not be anxious particularly about resources. That's not our part of the partnership with God. We commit to His vizion for our lives and He provides the resources we need, everything from inspiration and ideas, to the right people and capital.

> **Faith is a requirement for pleasing God in any capacity at all.**

Faith is a requirement for pleasing God in any capacity at all. Why do we think that we can survive as Christians with a base level of faith where we hope in salvation and eternal life and yet seem unable to trust our Father to resource what He's called us to do? I think for many of us, it's easier to believe in the salvation message than it is to trust God with our finances. Perhaps it is because death seems so far off, but our bills and our bank account have to be dealt with right now, today!

And without faith it is impossible to please God, because anyone who comes to him must believe that he exists and that he rewards those who earnestly seek him.

Hebrews 11:6 (NIV)

Faith is actually required for repentance as we see in Hebrews. If we come to Him in repentance, we first have to believe that He is and that He rewards those who earnestly seek Him. Faith is central to 2 Chronicles 7:14 by the very act of prayer and seeking. It's interesting to observe the various levels of trust we have, especially when it comes to resources for our vizion. We believe people will come and fill our churches every Sunday. We believe that we're called to be His witnesses. We believe that He wants people sent to the uttermost parts of the world to fulfill the Great Commission, and yet with our actions,

Selective faith and trust in God is worse than selective obedience because it tells God that He is not glorious.

we believe that it will be someone else who will be required to go, give and sacrifice. We believe God at the start of the capital campaign, but when the numbers don't come in like we think they should, we lose heart and close a project down. The truth is, we either believe God or we don't. We either walk out what He has called us to do or we do not. Selective faith and trust in God is worse than selective obedience because it tells God that He is not glorious, that somehow our circumstances are too big for Him and He is not worthy of our trust. He can send His only son, born of a virgin to live a sinless life, die a horrible death, be buried and rise again to take all of our sin, sickness, death and curse, but whatever crisis we're in is beyond Him.

The Glory of God is to reveal His nature to people, to show people what He is like, to be understood in and elementary sense. When we trust God in one circumstance but not another, we build a barrier in our relationship with God. We set up a boundary that will have to fall in order for us to have true and complete fellowship with Him. That is one of the very purposes of shaking. When God removes our self-imposed boundaries for Him, we have no choice but to trust and rely on Him in a deeper way. So we get on our knees, seek His face and cry out to Him and, of course, He answers! He's been there all along waiting for us!

Central to the story of God's love affair with man is man's reliance on Him and God's faithfulness to meet his every need. This theme is pervasive throughout Scripture both Old Testament and New. The Bible says, "He who trusts in His riches will fall." When? When the shaking occurs! If we are holding onto paper, when the

> **Trust is key to any relationship; without it, there is really no relationship at all. It's an empty promise of distant acquaintance.**

ground starts moving, we'll fall every time! That's why we need to have

100% reliance on Him, not on the numbers of people in our churches, not the trends in giving, not the success of our businesses or ministries, not the money in the bank account and not the value of our portfolios, – 100% TOTAL reliance on the Lord God Almighty

> **Faith comes by hearing and hearing by the word of God.**
>
> **Romans 10:17**

Without faith, we cannot complete the other steps in the restoration process. In all situations of recession that we have studied, faith plays a key role. We are completely dead in the water and stuck until we trust Him. We HAVE to trust Him and when we don't, He WILL shake us until we do; until we have no choice and He is proven faithful. Trust is key to any relationship; without it, there is really no relationship at all. It's an empty promise of distant acquaintance. With faith, we have the expectation that He will meet us in repentance. We have expectation that His grace covers all of our mistakes, that He rescues us, resources us and send us. We have the expectation of His grace, His unending favor and His extravagant love!

> **...take up the shield of faith with which you can extinguish all the flaming arrows of the evil one.**
>
> **Ephesians 6:16**

Faith is the shield that guards your heart and your dream from the attacks of doubt, insecurity, fatigue and failure. Faith will cause you to press on when it seems that hope is lost. Faith will drive you when nothing seems to be going your way. When there is no breakthrough in sight, no

> **Faith is the shield that guards your heart and your dream from the attacks of doubt, insecurity, fatigue and failure.**

job, no money, no resources and all your friends have left, faith will keep you alive.

"Faith without works is dead."

James 2:17

Faith is vizion. It's the sight, the conviction, the resolve and the assurance. It is the belief. Without it, there is no direction. Action is merely activity and life is without meaning. Without the conviction that you can accomplish something, commitment doesn't exist.

> **Faith is vizion**

Faith is what caused Moses to take the call from the burning bush to the courts of Pharaoh. Faith is what led the whole nation of Israel, to leave the comforts of Egypt, and the bondage there, to seek a nation of their own.

Faith is what caused the Israelites to renew their work on the temple in Haggai. It's also what drove Nehemiah to pray and fast, approach the king with a sad face and to ask boldly for provisions to return to Jerusalem to rebuild the wall. It's what caused the inhabitants of Jerusalem under Nehemiah's direction to complete the work in 52 days despite intense opposition and what fueled the rending of the hearts in the book of Joel.

Faith motivates; it moves you, it propels you to take action, to be a catalyst of change and an instrument of transformation. What mountain, obstacle, trial or terror can stand in the face of one with complete trust in God and the faith to speak to the circumstances around him and tell them to be in alignment with the will of God?

> *...the God who gives life to the dead and who calls things that are not as though they were.*
>
> **Romans 4:17**

Obedience

And this is love: that we walk in obedience to his
commands. As you have heard from the beginning,
his command is that you walk in love.

2 John 1:6

Obedience is love to God. Without it, there is a lack of trust, a lack of understanding or just plain rebellion. His will is clear. It's all through Scripture even at a very basic level. His will is that we go and make disciples of all nations. There is no ambiguity, no question whether it applies to you or not. It's for all of us, in its entirety. It's an encouragement, an admonishment, the last words of Jesus on this earth, a command to be sure, but above all, an expression of our love to God. Have you ever wanted to be part of something big, really, really BIG? If you knew of the biggest project on earth, would you want to be a part of it? What if the fate of literally billions of people hung in the balance? Would there be anything more important? We have all been *personally* invited to be part of the largest rescue effort in human history. Jesus invited us to "…go, and make disciples of all nations…" an invitation far too many take lightly. Have you ever thought, "What would it take to actually fulfill this mandate in our lifetime, in this generation?"

> **What if we could actually fulfill the Great Commission in our lifetime?**

Imagine the amount of resources it

will take to accomplish this? We need people from all backgrounds, in all fields, from all walks of life to accomplish it. We need the wealth of nations to cover the expenses, and think of the coordination that will have to occur! It will be nothing short of the most massive mobilization and logistics effort EVER! But it's more than logistics and mobilization, it takes repentance, faith, obedience and unity. It takes the commitment of all Christ followers, a realization of what their part is and obedience to playing their role.

The commands of God are not hard to discern or hidden deep in Scripture. They are readily apparent in His life and message. He called us all, every single Christian to be an active part of fulfilling the Great Commission. By accepting our call and coming into obedience to it, we open ourselves up to be more fulfilled than we have ever been. We also position ourselves in the center of the flow of resources that the Lord is pouring out to complete His work.

> *"But seek first the Kingdom of God and His righteousness and all these things will be added unto you."*
>
> **Matthew 6:33 (NIV)**

Vizion

How do we seek first His kingdom? By doing what He said. It starts with a personal, all-out commitment to the Great Commission and is lived out daily through the pursuit of the call of God on our life; our purpose, destiny or vizion. To disciple nations is something we all need to personalize.

God told Isaiah, before I formed you, I knew you. God took a dream He had for the world and created a person around it. He included all the passion, gifts, talents, abilities and insights that would be needed to

> **To disciple nations is something we all need to personalize.**

make that dream happen. We can know with confidence that what God called us to do, He has given us the ability to make happen and will flow the favor, connections and resources to us that we need to fulfill it.

Once we are committed to the Great Commission and know what our calling is, we begin to have a really good idea of what we need to be in obedience to. As we pursue God's purpose for our life, He will bring us all the pieces we need. It's not just some grand idea, our vizion, it is a

> ***Vizion*** = dream, God's dream for you, the purpose for which you were created.

mandate on our life. You may say, "God's called me to be a writer but I don't know why, I'm not very confident in my ability." It's not really a choice. We either do what we're created for and live the life He designed for us, or our life is other than what it was meant to be, something less.

Audacity of Faith

Because of fear, insecurity or perceived lack, people choose not to be who they were created to be. It is audacious of us to think that we have an option! If God has called us to be something great, who are we to determine whether that is what WE want for our lives? This is the audacity of pride and rebellion. Living a life other than what we are intended is disobedience, and so is not finding out what we are called to be.

What we need is the audacity of faith; an unwavering faith in God our Father, Daddy-God, who has created us, has our best interests in mind, has a plan for our lives and is committed to the success of that plan with us. Faith shows us that we are not alone, that God has commissioned us and that He is in control of the outcome. We are responsible to wholeheartedly pursue our vizion and He provides the rest: from opportunity to connections and resources.

When we step out and commit to our vizion, even though we have no idea how it can happen or even what all the pieces are to make it happen, we will see God move on our behalf. It's our purpose; it's the design of our life. It's our destiny! When we're pursuing it, we're in our zone, we're doing what we're called to do and we'll find that things start happening. We'll find ourselves saying, "I'm getting provided for, I'm stepping out, it's uncomfortable but God's bringing me people that believe in me and things are moving. Whatever I need God is taking care of for me." We will see more happen as we step out into our calling than before when we were just sitting on the sidelines, floating through life. Welcome to the Grand Adventure!

Goals & Objectives

By personalizing the Great Commission and finding out what our vizion is and how it fits in, we will begin to provide ourselves a road map for our life, but this is not enough. We are not called to start obedience, but to see it through. Now it's time to put together a set of directions that will take us there. This happens through mapping out goals and objectives.

Obedience means taking action

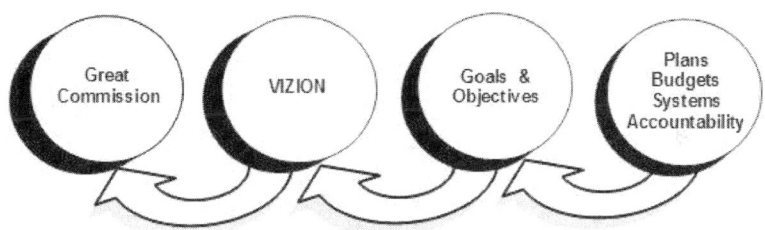

If we believe God has called us to be a missionary doctor in Africa, in support of the Great Commission, then we need to set a goal to become a doctor. We need to pick a medical school, apply, get funding and get to work. If God has called us to be an actor, make a portfolio, take some acting classes and move to New York or LA. Once we know our vizion and we fully commit to it, the next steps become pretty obvious – just get started!

An objective is a step in the process towards the completion of our vizion. To go to medical school, one first has to apply. To be an actor, one needs a portfolio. Objectives map out the major milestones so we know what needs to be done.

A goal is a quantifiable, measurable, achievable task with a time frame for

> A **goal** is a quantifiable, measurable, achievable task with a time frame for completion.

completion. It's a commitment. It's the point that thoughts and dreams for our lives become dates on our calendars and entries in our checkbook. It's where real obedience happens. If we want to write a book, we have to sit down and do it, we can't just talk about it. Achieving goals takes discipline and sacrifice; they are the fuel behind the passion and the dream.

Plans, Budgets, Systems & Accountability

Owning the Great Commission, finding our vizion and setting goals and objectives are all big steps, but where the rubber meets the road are plans, budgets, systems and accountability. This is where our vizion meets the daily grind. This is the time when the team is formed, the money is allocated, the deadlines are laid out, time is managed, resources are delineated and action is taken. This is where the micro meets the macro, where strategy gives way to tactics. A General can't win a war with broad-stroke strategy. He needs men on the ground; systems to supply those men, budgets to pay for those supplies and communications to ensure things end up at their intended destination. This is where our involvement in making disciples of nations goes from a fluffy, green & purple unicorn kind of concept to "What am I going to do today? I'm going to balance my checkbook." Why? Because that's a system I need in place to be able to manage my finances, to be able to get out of debt, to go to medical school, to be a doctor, to be a missionary in Africa, to support the Great Commission. See how it all fits together? Now we know what we're doing on a day-in day-out basis to be obedient to our calling.

Plans

This is the point where there has to be a shift from a discussion on Biblical economics to an application on practical economics. A plan is a specific set of steps leading to the accomplishment of a goal. If we want to get out of debt, we need a plan. First, we need to evaluate what resources we need and then

> A **plan** is a specific set of steps leading to the accomplishment of a goal.

write down actions, milestones and potential challenges, being as detailed as possible. Then we must have accountability and daily/weekly actions items.

Nehemiah had a plan laid out when he approached the king. He had spent months fasting and praying about the vizion and had thought out the details. The king asked him how long he would be gone, so he set a time. He asked him for letters of safe passage through the neighboring nations and for access to the king's forest for lumber to make the beams for the gates of the citadel by the temple, for the city wall and for the residence that he would occupy. God gave him great favor with the king, but prior to the favor, he had done his homework. He allowed God to speak to his heart, owned the vizion, sought God in depth through prayer and fasting, committed to it, developed a plan and then stepped out.

Plans rely heavily on budgets and systems. All three work together, along with accountability, which helps the whole objective stay on track. To have a good plan, we have to have a system and a budget that will produce the results, or meet the goal we are planning to achieve.

The first step in developing a workable plan is to define the goal we are trying to achieve. Just like our goals and objectives fit into our vizion, so a plan will be the specific steps (systems, budget, accountability and action items) we will put in place to achieve that goal.

God gave Moses a plan for approaching Pharaoh. He told him about the plagues, and different tactics to prove the power of God was with Him. He told him what to tell the Israelites when asked who sent him. He even laid out the plan for the mass Exodus and how to gather provisions for the journey, thus plundering Egypt as they left. There was a very detailed plan laid out by God on Mount Sinai for the construction of the tabernacle and all its various pieces, instruments and furnishings. They had a plan as well, for the reconstruction of the temple in Haggai. It's all part of the model of action taken in obedience to the vizion God placed in them.

Budgets

Not a lot of people I know really like budgeting. I'm a numbers guy and I don't like it. How come? Because most of the time a budget shows us where our financial mess is and what we don't have. It helps us to set limits we don't want to be tied to and shows us where we lack discipline.

> A **budget** is a plan for managing financial resources.

Well that's one way of looking at it. Here's another way:

A budget is a strategy to expedite the accomplishment of God's dream for your life.

Can we achieve success without a budget? Possibly, but it's a lot like trying to get in shape without working out. If we like delay in our life, if we like waiting, if we enjoy the heartsick position of deferred hope, then we don't budget. But **IF** we have a dream we're serious about and we want to see God rapidly move in our financial life, we might want to get this part down.

Habakkuk 2 talks about writing the vision down and making it plain that a herald may run with it. The plan had to be communicated to all ends of the kingdom so everyone would know about it. It had to be plainly written so all aspects of the socio-economic scale could understand it and take part. A budget is a very plainly written implementation tool for a vizion. Could someone convict us of pursuing our dream merely by looking at our checkbook?

> **A budget is your financial prayer strategy.**

Our budget is our financial prayer strategy. Have we ever thought about it like that? It will show us where our debt is and how, once that debt is gone, we can invest more in our calling. So write it down and begin praying into it. Father, give me wisdom and a strategy to pay off my car so I can invest the $350 a month in my vizion. God honors our planning. He appreciates our work, sowing into what He has called us to do. Budgeting is repentance, faith and obedience actively walked out.

Moses had a very detailed budget for the tabernacle project. We know that specifically because the needs are so meticulously laid out that the craftsmen went to Moses in Exodus 36:6-7 and told him that they had

> Budgeting is repentance, faith and obedience actively walked out.

"...more than enough to complete the work." They knew when they had met their budget!

It starts with His vizion for the world. He burdens us with our piece in that vizion and then asks for our faith and obedience; then, He resources us. Budgeting is managing these resources correctly. It's like a piping system through which blessing and more resources can flow. Once the system is set in place, no matter how much more He blesses us, we know how to manage it. Nothing is wasted, everything is used for His kingdom. His Word goes forth, people are touched and lives are changed. It's that simple.

In Ezra, prior to the 50,000 Jews returning to Jerusalem at Cyrus' order, they asked their neighbors for provisions for the trip. Additionally, several kings of Persia provided for the journey of the Jews, the building of the temple and the sacrifices to be made there. King Artaxerxes actually outlines a budget to the Governors of the Trans-Euphrates as to what they need to pay for the maintenance of the activities of the temple in Jerusalem.

Now I, King Artaxerxes, decree that all the treasurers of Trans-Euphrates are to provide with diligence whatever Ezra the priest, the teacher of the Law of the God of heaven, may ask of you— up to a hundred talents of silver, a hundred cords of wheat, a hundred baths of wine, a hundred baths of olive oil, and salt

> *without limit. Whatever the God of heaven has*
> *prescribed, let it be done with diligence for the temple*
> *of the God of heaven. Why should his wrath fall on*
> *the realm of the king and of his sons?*

Ezra 7:21-23

Are there challenges in our budget? Have we made mistakes? Maybe we have too much debt, too much spending, and not enough savings? This is what we must take to God and repent of. This is what we, in faith, believe that God is going to help us restore. Then we come into obedience by going after the vision God called us to, and reflecting those priorities in our budget. The grace and redemptive love of God does not absolve us of our responsibility to manage His resources, which are under our care, correctly. In fact they are the reasons why we change and transform the patterns of our lives.

I believe God will intervene in dramatic ways in people's lives when they pull out their mess and say to Him, "Here it is. Help!" In fact, I know it! I've seen it! We may not have plans to get out of debt, or know how to deal with our budget; we may be on the verge of filing bankruptcy or about to lose our house. By turning from our mistakes and towards His grace, having faith that He will reward us for diligently seeking Him, finding our vizion and committing to what He has called us to do, and walking it out in obedience, we will see transformation in our life and finances.

In Haggai, from the day that they came into obedience and began to work, God told them He was with them. God will prove Himself faithful in our finances as we are "strong and do the work". Budgeting is the work! He will begin to bless us and show us how to have extra discretionary income, how to leverage it to pay off debt, how we can do things differently that are going to allow us to reach our goals, objectives and vision. So be strong and do the work.

Systems

A system is a procedure, process, platform or method that helps us achieve a goal. Simply put, systems are ways of doing things. We need a good financial system to track our money, pay our bills and invest in the things that are important to us. How much are we investing in the vision God has given us? Do we have a system to get out of debt so we can invest and give more?

> A **system** is a procedure, process, platform or method that helps us achieve a goal.

There are simple systems observed all throughout the Biblical models. We see the system for raising money in Exodus, the system for collecting freewill offerings for the building the tabernacle project. We see a system in Joel for gathering all the people and crying out to God in prayer and fasting. Even in Haggai, they had systems for the construction of the temple. In many cases, the workings of these systems are not included in great detail in the text.

In rebuilding the wall of Jerusalem, Nehemiah put many systems in place. Some are mentioned in the Bible; others are inferred. The overall vizion is described in Chapters 2 & 3.

Vizion – to rebuild Jerusalem's Wall

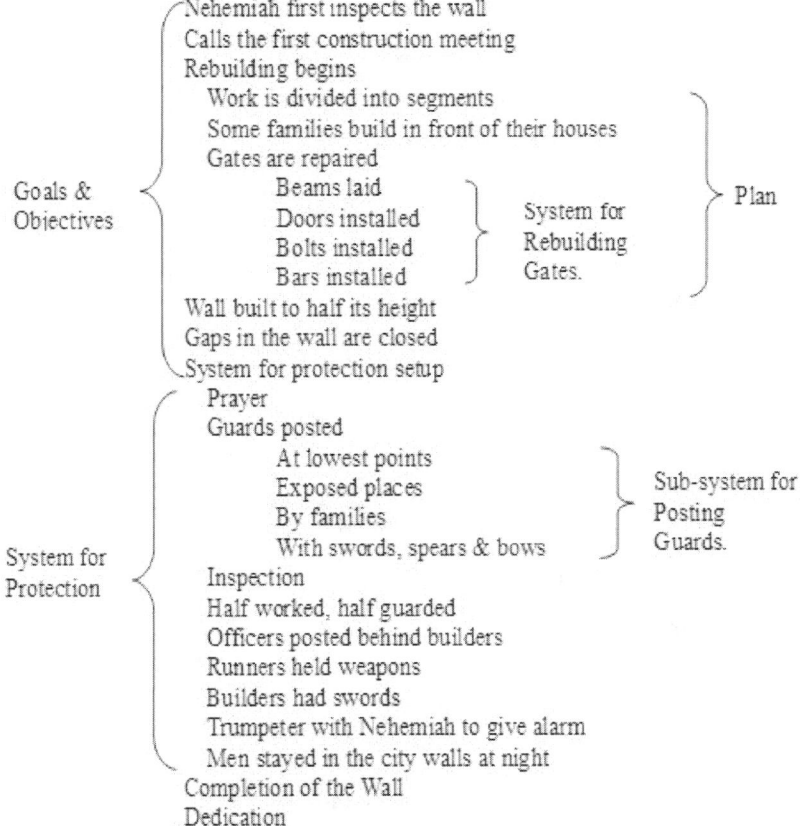

You can see how the vizion of rebuilding the wall comes together. The goals and objectives are the main steps. The systems are processes for the more detailed pieces and then there are even sub-systems for the really detailed portions. This was a massive coordination effort and much had to happen in many places at once to pull it off. Budgeting came into play in Nehemiah 5 when the Israelites raised a cry of protest against the nobles and officials for charging usury on the mortgages and loans they were providing. Nehemiah implemented a God-given strategy to cancel the loan interest, loan principal and for the restoration of the homes and lands back to their rightful owners.

In the same way, we need to have the vizion written down plainly so that we have a course to run on. Writing down a goal and the practical steps to achieve it is Biblical and part of obedience. We need to see how our goals, plans, systems and budgets are laid out so we know how they all fit together from the big picture to the daily activities. Here is a diagram for a sample plan with systems, to get out of debt.

Vizion – get out of debt

```
Determine debt (balances, rates & monthly payments)  ⟹ Make the vision plain
Prioritize debt      ⟹ Goals & Objectives
      ⎧ Write a budget
      ⎪       Determine income                    ⎫
      ⎪       Determine monthly expenses          ⎬ Budgeting system
      ⎪       Determine discretionary income      ⎭
      ⎪ Retire each debt
      ⎪       Plan for debt pay downs             ⎫
      ⎪       Resources needed                    ⎪
      ⎪       Potential challenges                ⎬ System for paying off individual debts
      ⎪       Accountability                      ⎪
      ⎪       Weekly/Daily Action items           ⎭
Plan  ⎨           Balancing checkbook
      ⎪               Record all deposits                    ⎫
      ⎪               Record all checks and withdrawals      ⎬ System
      ⎪               Periodically reconcile with account    ⎭
      ⎪           Paying bills monthly
      ⎪               Place bills in a central location  ⎫
      ⎪               Write checks/online banking        ⎪
      ⎪               Update register and POA&M           ⎬ System
      ⎪               Apply extra payments via POA&M      ⎭
      ⎪           Giving
      ⎩ Update progress of plan - Accountability
```

This illustrates the planning that it takes to really attack a vizion. See how all the pieces of plans, budgets, system and accountability work together? There is coordination required to make a vision or goal come to pass. Once we've mapped it out we can see exactly what the steps are and the pieces we need in place on a daily basis. These systems begin to integrate into our life. This is where behavior is changed. New habits are developed and transformation occurs.

Transformation is a many-faceted process. It starts with saturating our minds and hearts with the Word and the presence of God. This alone will change our hearts. We see God is for us, that He has showered us with His grace and it is His nature to rescue, resource and send us. As our hearts change, our desires and priorities change to align with His. Our focus is renewed and begins to shift from a self-centered life to a Great Commission life. With our focus on His plan for the world, He shares with us His purpose for us – our vizion. As we commit to the vizion and run hard after it, the details become clear, the resources are evidenced and our goals are accomplished. Our lives change in this process and transformation happens.

Accountability

Have you ever taken an easier job, run after the money or settled for less? Did you ever date the wrong person, knowing they weren't God's best for you? Have you walked away from relationships or perhaps a church that challenged you because you didn't want to hear it anymore?

I'm tired of making sacrifices and being broke! I'm tired of not having the things that I want! I'm tired of being single, lonely, cold, tired, depressed! I want to be blessed, I want a family, I don't want to work in the trenches anymore and I just want a normal life! Have any of us ever felt this way?

The Israelites did in Haggai. King Cyrus allowed 50,000 Jews to go back to Jerusalem and rebuild the Temple. Hey, we're done being slaves in a foreign land; that's cool, let's go home! Who wouldn't want that? What they didn't understand was when they got home and the real work starts. We've got to dig a hole today, we've got to dig a trench tomorrow and we've got to lay the foundation. We've got to make bricks. We have to put one brick on top of another. It's sweaty work, man! It's the grimy, in the dirt, mundane stuff that nobody cares about.

> **It's the decisions we make on a day-to-day basis in the trenches that determines our character, our future, our vizion and ultimately our legacy.**

They laid the foundation of the temple, working on building it for two years and then stopped. God let them for a time. He watched them to see what they would do. They had a clear directive. It's the decisions we make on a day-to-day basis in the trenches that determines our character, our future, our vizion and ultimately our legacy.

They woke up one day and realized everything was gone. Drought and famine had happened. Recession occurred. No water, no food. Where is God? How could this happen? God was saying, "Now, are you going to do what I told you to do?" God didn't move and neither did His resources. He's not schizophrenic, He hadn't changed His mind and their calling; it was the same!

"Okay, God. You win." they said. Forget our houses, we'll go back to work and they went back to work. Interesting thing is, God restored their resources too. Recession ended. Lesson learned.

Did you ever have a dream that you knew you were called to and it got too hard? Did you quit or walk away from your calling, your vizion? One of the awesome things about God is He doesn't give up on us.

> *...for God's gifts and His call are irrevocable.*
> **Romans 11:29**

Another version of this verse says, "...for the gifts and call of God are without repentance." God is not going to repent of what He called us to do because it gets hard. He also doesn't let us off the hook because we quit. He pursues us when we run away. He gets our attention and brings us back into our purpose and destiny – vizion.

This is where the recession comes in, do you remember? So how do we avoid getting off track again? Accountability. Accountability is responsibility to someone for the performance of an activity. It's peer-review. It's having people in our life who will "call us" on our stuff when we get off-track and it's something we all desperately need!

Accountability is critical in this process of sustained change or true transformation.

> **Accountability** is responsibility to someone for the performance of an activity.

We can't do this walk alone. We're not designed to anyway. We need others around us to walk with us, to remind us of what we have committed to, and to help us through when times get tough. It requires relationship. We have to have other people, not just working side-by-side with us, but being in our lives, up in our business, in the details. It can be uncomfortable. None of us likes to be held to a higher level, or called on our stuff when we fall short. But it's good for us. It keeps us on track and it can help recession-proof our life!

Who is someone in your life you trust enough to share your vizion with and be accountable to?

Move!

I have a close friend of mine who knew God had called him to be an actor. He and I went out to dinner one night. John is like a brother to me and I had always encouraged him to follow his dream. We lived in Ohio together and were on the church drama team. We started talking about purpose and calling.

I told him. "John, God didn't call you to be an actor, that's the dumbest thing I've ever heard, what a waste of your time and talent. You're going to go make Hollywood movies? Yeah right!" Needless to say, John was pretty upset.

"You're like my best friend, how can you say that?" He replied.

"I'm just telling you, John, I'm tired of playing with you. I'm just going to be real! Give it up. You're an engineer, stay in Toledo and work for the auto industry."

See, John had talked about his acting career for years, but hadn't done much to make his dream happen other than participate in the church drama program. I believed in John and knew he had what it took to really make a go of it, but he had to commit, fully commit! This particular night, I wanted to see how much he really believed in his dream.

John got ticked, which is what I wanted. I wanted to see if he would really defend his dream. Finally he stood up from the table and said,

"No, I really think I'm supposed to..." I cut him off mid-sentence,

"John, you're wrong. You're not going to be an actor, that's stupid. God wouldn't call anybody to be an actor. There's nothing important about acting."

By this time he wouldn't sit down anymore at all, he was starting to make his stand.

"No, no, I really think..."

I cut him off again, "See? You think? You're not even convinced! You don't know, you don't know what you're supposed to do with your life. You've got an engineering degree, John, go be an engineer!"

By this time, I was on my feet too. Pushing him harder. I knew it would take something dramatic to shake him up and cause him to do what he needed to do. The next part of his dream was going to be a big step and he had to know that he knew it was right. He stepped closer to me and he got more confident. He got right up in my face,

"I know what I'm supposed to do and this is it. I'm supposed to be an actor!"

He was almost yelling at this point.

I stepped into his space and grabbed him by his shirt and I pulled his face right next to mine and I said

"Then Move! Because you can't do it here in Toledo, Ohio!"

John got the message. He reeled back a bit like he was just hit right between the eyes. We sat back down and finished dinner. We talked about setting a goal, a date for his big move to LA. A couple of weeks later, John announced to me that he had done it. He set a goal to move July 1st. Three months later, John did it! He moved to L.A. It was the first big goal towards realizing his vizion.

We have a calling too; we have a responsibility to obey God and make it happen. Only in America do we think that our calling is something that we have the audacity to choose. If God's called us to be an actor, a musician, a CEO or a business leader and we're feeling not really sure, remember this; if we don't do what we're called to do we're not being who we were designed to be.

Go do what God told you to do; and that means move! John did. His first goal was getting to a place where he could work as an actor. Now he's taking acting classes with the best people in the industry, he's going to auditions, he has his portfolio together and he's done some work in the field. There are starts and stops along the way, but he's there, he's working on his dream. He is on task with His calling and now God can bring to him all the things he needs to get it done. He already met his wife in LA on a train heading to work one morning. It's interesting how God brings you everything you need as you step out in active obedience.

Where are you? Are you convinced of your calling? Will you move?

Unity and Releasing

Pretty much every person that I've talked to about their dream feels at some level inadequate. If we don't, chances are our vizion is too small! Vizion is not something we do alone.

Unity

Part of the character of the relational God that created us is that He wants us to live and work together. That's how He designed us. Taking personal ownership of the Great Commission will cause us immediately to look outside of ourselves for help; and even our piece in that is too big for just us to handle. We are not designed to work our vizion alone.

> **We are not designed to work our vizion alone.**

Bringing discipleship to nations is not something any one person, denomination, group, nation, race or association can handle on its own. We need everyone operating in their purpose and destiny. This is one of those areas where the wheels seem to fall off the cart. We know we need each other to reach the world, and yet how many of us personally, with our churches, our businesses and our ministries are linked together globally? We all know the power that was evident at the launching of the early church and that it came through unity, but are we willing to put aside differences and wholeheartedly run after God together?

As a business guy, this is one thing that truly frustrates me. In order to succeed in business, we have to work with others. We are constantly connecting, networking and looking at joint ventures and projects together. What I see in the church world is that this doesn't happen as much, and certainly not on any consistent level that will get the job done. We need to rise up as the men and women that God called us to be, pray for one another, lift each other up, work together and live, in unity!

I was invited to be part of a city wide Pastors' prayer meeting once a week—most of the time we had a dozen or so people there. I work in church financing and interact with many Pastors and through our conversations I had heard of several other unity movements that existed for a while, but never seemed to get off the ground. One week we were talking about scheduling a day of prayer and fasting for our city. It was mentioned, that maybe we should do this once a quarter. God had me studying in Haggai and Joel at the time and I couldn't help but think, "If we had 25% unemployment in this city, we would be praying and fasting a bit more often!"

His people are created for His Glory to bring honor to His name and we do that by coming together to take His message to all nations. If we are

> **His people are created for His Glory to bring honor to His name and we do that by coming together to take His message to all nations.**

not individually and corporately working with a coordinated effort around the world to complete the task, then how serious are we about getting the job done? This puts in question the level of repentance, faith and obedience that we really have. Coming together in unity, one body, many parts, in a vine and branches sort of way is a basic and foundational message of the Gospel and one we have to demonstrate to the world. It's not just a good idea; we simply CAN NOT complete our task and remain in obedience to God without it! This is something we have to get right!

We were designed to be together, not segregated in different churches across our lands. The divisions of race, denomination, political affiliation, status and whatever else, are man-made divisions not the God-made variety, as some believe. Expressions of worship can come in many forms and take on many different tones, all of which are pleasing to God. The worship of our lives, though, needs to be a corporate one. We can't do what He has called us to do in the Sunday morning boxes where many of us live. If He has to, He'll shake the very foundations of the institutions we have come to rely on. In fact, I think that shaking has already begun.

Biblical Unity

During the Exodus, it took the massive effort of moving several million people out of one nation into the desert and ultimately to the Promised Land. At Mount Sinai, when God gave Moses the plan for building the tabernacle, they needed donations of all the materials, but even more than that, they needed the skilled workers,

> *Then Moses summoned Bezalel and Oholiab and*
> *every skilled person to whom the LORD had given*
> *ability and who was willing to come and do the work.*

They received from Moses all the offerings the
Israelites had brought to carry out the work of
constructing the sanctuary. And the people
continued to bring freewill offerings morning after
morning.

Exodus 36:2, 3

In Nehemiah 2, he shares the vizion of rebuilding the wall with the people and tells them of all the favor he received from the king in sending him back to Jerusalem. One group or family could not rebuild the wall on their own, but upon sharing the vizion, the people bought in and were stirred to help in this massive task. The project took all the different trades and different kinds of people all willing to work. The priests, the goldsmith, the perfume-maker, the rulers, the sons and the daughters all rebuilt pieces of the wall. There are a lot of people who don't sound very significant. In several places a family rebuilt the section of the wall directly in front of where they lived.

So if we don't know what our piece is yet, what's directly in front of us? Our vision! We see what's directly in front of us and if we would build the wall directly in front of us, then the whole city comes up. If we want to fulfill the Great Commission, we need to do what's right in front of us, which is our vision and our piece. What is on our heart that needs to be changed, who needs helped, what can be done better for the Glory of His name in the earth?

For some people it's "Wells in Africa." For others it's the mission field, still others, it is business. Whatever it is, our piece is our vizion. It's what's directly in front of us. Work alongside those who are next to you. We can't work just by ourselves. Our vizion will be expanded to help other people reach their vizion. We'll be leveraging our time and efforts and accomplishing more.

Do we want to disciple others? Find out what God has called them to do. Maybe we'll have somebody that wants to build a building. We might have someone else that wants to

> **We can't complete our vizion on our own. We will have to have partners. God designed it that way. No one person builds the temple. No one person rebuilt the wall. It's everybody working together.**

launch missions. We might have someone that's called to be a human resource director for the body of Christ, where they can interview people all day and help them find out what they are passionate about, what their job skills are and what their resume looks like. If we could help people find the piece right in front of them and encourage them to go out and do it; we will activate them in the body of Christ.

Once somebody gets activated they see that they don't have to go to Africa to be part of discipling nations. We don't have to sell everything and live in a hut somewhere to help fulfill the Great Commission. We get excited. It's freeing! We could simply be an equipper or an exhorter. My mom takes care of old, dying people and writes devotions for other caretakers. That's her ministry, that's part of her piece, that's what she's passionate about doing. It's not something I am called to, but there's a huge need for it. When people get on board with their call there's excitement and a true sense of purpose.

Whatever excuses we've had for staying in our paneled houses, they aren't going to fly much longer. The Lord is raising up a movement of people who will do what He has called us all to do, and do it together, methodically and in unity. Do not miss this opportunity to be involved in what the He is doing in the earth right now! Some of the most significant happenings in the history of the church are taking place right now, and as Christians, God has called US all to be a part of it!

Releasing

Resources, blessing and anointing all flow from one source to another. Interconnectivity that needs to happen as part of unity is the flowing one to another. The concept of flowing is what we call releasing. It's a concept that goes way beyond giving.

All throughout Scripture, money is described as flowing like water.

> *Restore our fortunes Oh Lord, like streams in the*
> *Negev.*
>
> **Psalm 126:4**

'Flow resources to us, God,' is what this Psalm says. Flowing is much like a stream, a river or an ocean. There is no lack. Releasing is the giving of ourselves as well as of our resources. It is what some would call being fully expressed. It's giving, but it's more. It's working in our passion and gifting, but it's more than that too. It's best described in the concepts of flowing.

When we understand that money, talent, gifting, love and anointing flows like water, we can begin to understand the idea of releasing. We can't hold water in our hands. It's not designed that way. The waters in Genesis covered the earth. They are designed to flow freely. So are our gifts, talents, abilities, money and resources. They're designed to be part of a continuous flow.

As resources are poured out on us, we are designed to pour them out on others. The more we pour out, the more flows to us. It's like a river. As the river flows downstream, it creates a vacuum upstream, causing more water to flow to the vacuum. It actually attracts or draws more water to the place from which it flowed. As we pour out, the resources of God flow to us in a mightier way causing our needs to be met and overflowing to be poured out further. People that truly understand this principle realize that they can't out give God. The more we pour out, the more that flows to us. It's momentum - flow. It's scientific, yes, but it's also very spiritual. It's a deep concept.

Go to a river and try to pick it up. Try to take it home or hold onto it. It can never work. It's not designed that way. If we could pick up a portion of a river, what would

> **The more we pour out, the more flows to us. It's like a river. As the river flows downstream, it creates a vacuum upstream, causing more water to flow to the vacuum. It actually attracts or draws more water to the place from which it flowed.**

happen? The surrounding water would rush into the lowest point and fill up that which is lacking. We can't leave a hole in a river! The same is true about finances, or any kind of gift that we pour out in obedience to God. It's true about love as well. The more we pour out, the more comes back to us. It's simply a law; it's the way God designed things. He showed us in nature and even pointed to it over and over again in the Bible so we could understand it.

When we try to hold onto our resources it doesn't work. It stagnates the resources and spoils the container. If we could pick up a river, what would be left are small pools of water, stagnate pools that are only good for killing fish and breeding mosquitoes and disease—and either way they stink.

This is what happens to water when it is restricted. Look at what happens to resources when they are bottled up and hoarded. It causes the hoarder to rot. It breeds greed, selfishness, paranoia and the like. It causes hardness of heart and makes it hard for the rich person to enter the kingdom. This is why Jesus told the rich, young ruler to give away all he had and follow him. He walked away sad because he couldn't do it. What he didn't realize was that if he had given it all away, he would have gained so much more than he had to begin with. He didn't understand the principles of flow and releasing.

The best way to look at it is like this: the Lord Almighty is pouring out His resources on the earth like a giant river to fulfill the work He has called us to. No one can hold the river, which is why He didn't call this mission to be funded by the World Bank or the Federal Reserve. He wants us all in the flow; set free and resourced to do the work He has called us to. It's a maximally inclusive Gospel requiring the efforts of every single person and family. No one is exempt. How deep in this river are we willing to go? How much of the Lord Almighty's work and provision do we want to be a part of?

To break the back of the recession, we need to restart the flow. Governments and administrations understand this; they just don't know how to do it effectively. Placing hundreds of billions of dollars in the hands of the banks and institutions that had a major part in creating the recession we are in did not work. The thought was, with this glut of resources, banks would flow to businesses and restart the economy. When they took their cash out of the system and held on to incredibly large cash reserves, it actually made things worse. Without understanding these God-birthed concepts and ideas, they will try several different things, many of which make the problems worse, and then when God relents and has mercy on His people, they claim success, which perpetuates a lack of understanding.

Biblical Releasing

The disciples got it. They saw Jesus as the source. Think about it, when he called Peter and Andrew, they were out fishing. They had been out the entire day and had caught almost nothing. Jesus walked up and told them to go out one more time and cast their nets on the other side. They took a risk and listened even though they knew how to fish and were experts in technique, the waters they were fishing and the whole process. It was their livelihood! When they obeyed, it took them two boats to haul in all the fish. After they finally brought it all in, Jesus said, "*Come and follow me and I will make you fishers of men.*" They dropped their nets and followed him. (Luke 5:1-11) Do you think they understood something about the source of their blessing? They knew where the flow came from!

True understanding of this principle will cause us to give radically; of ourselves, our talents, our time, our resources and all that we have. As we release, God causes more to flow to us. It is critical in the process of fulfilling your vizion. We need resources to do what the Lord has called us to do: real estate resources, equipment resources, financial resources and human resources. The more we release, the more flows to us. The true embracing of this concept causes people to give cheerfully and extravagantly. It is freeing to know that we can't out give God!

To release is to resource. It's the pathway to go from a position of poverty to a position of provision and promise. This is another reason why unity is so important. If we are connected with others and working with them in the fulfillment of the Great Commission, we can see and know their needs. We have opportunity to release to them resources that God gave us, and thus the flow continues. In Exodus, the Israelites had the abundance of Egypt flow into their hands. Those who were willing and whose hearts moved them gave of that abundance to the building of the tabernacle. With the tabernacle built, God had a place where He physically dwelt with man. He led them into their promised land – a land *flowing* with milk and honey.

In the Haggai model, God had flowed resources to the Israelites so they could return to Jerusalem and build the temple. He also provided all they needed to get it done. As He flowed resources to them for their trip back from Babylon, they flowed as human resources to the work on the temple. When they stopped the flow after two years and only having laid the foundation, God stopped the flow of abundance to them through an economic recession (drought and famine). Once they repented and began to flow their time and skill, renewing their work on the temple, the flow of resources to them was restarted or unblocked.

In the story of Nehemiah, God put His desire in the heart of His servant who was cupbearer to the king. As Nehemiah stepped out with a plan and in obedience to God, the resources of the king were released to him. He traveled back to Jerusalem, rallied the people and began work on the wall. As the people gave of their time and skill, God saw fit to flow to them

> **Resources R4 Vizion**
> Repentance
> Faith
> Obedience
> Unity
> Releasing

more financial resources by releasing them from the debt they owed. I believe, one of the main reasons, if not THE primary reason God moved Nehemiah's heart to return and rebuild the wall was so He would release the people from the debt they were in. It wasn't about the wall. God was rescuing them and resourcing them after they had been sent to do His bidding.

The releasing of resources doesn't just happen all by itself. Resources are designed for a particular purpose. God is a God of order and He makes things for a reason. Resources are for vizion; or as we like to say, resources R4 vizion. The releasing is the final step in every Biblical model that we discussed. All of the stories were different and had many twists and turns to them. Some started in slavery and exile, others in blessing and prosperity. The common thread in all of them is this pattern we see of repentance, faith, obedience, unit and releasing (R4).

We say that resources R4 vizion. God funds you, provides for you or resources you, whether it's connection or ability or whatever you need. He gives us all the pieces to build our piece of the wall. We may be the guy making the bricks. We may be the person with the plumb line. You may be the one setting the bricks in their place. You may be somebody in the back that's just handing out the mortar. It doesn't matter. We're all still building the wall. Our piece is vital and we are needed! If everyone does his piece the wall gets built. It all works together.

God funds His vision. Rick Warren, author of the *Purpose Driven Life* says "Stop asking God to bless what you're doing, get on board with what He is doing, because He's already blessing that!" I love the account of Joshua meeting with the Angel of the Lord just before Jericho. Joshua encounters a man standing with a drawn sword and asks a very human question,

"Are you for us or for our enemies?"

You have to love the response,

"Neither" he replied, "but as commander of the army of the Lord I have now come." a very God-like response. The question is not "Will God bless what we are doing?" but rather, are we part of what He is blessing,

His will, what He is doing? (Joshua 5:13-15)

When God does a thing, he doesn't slack. When He created the world He put in plenty of lumber, gold, diamonds, oil, etc. He did the same thing on every major building project. He blessed Abraham to birth a family and blessed His people (during the Exodus) to birth a nation. He provided abundant resources to build the tabernacle, build the temple, rebuild the wall, rebuild the temple and even launch His first church plant. We're talking about resources on every level from the personal to corporate, from project financing to capital campaigns.

Why Resources

So we know that God resources His vision and that He resources abundantly. As we give careful thought to our ways, the question becomes "Why would He resource you?" Are you doing

> **Why would God resource you?**

what He's called you to? Do you know what your purpose is, not just your want or desire, but God's dream for you? I call a God-dream a vizion. A vizion is a God-given destiny or calling that is part of His grand plan to share His love with the world and make His name glorious. We all have a part in it.

A great place to start is to look at the heart of God. What is He passionate about? He has a heart for the world. Jesus lays out the plan in what is widely known as the Great Commission.

Jesus referred to His body as the temple when He told the Pharisees, *"...destroy this temple and I will raise it again in three days."* So if His body is literally the temple, than that is what we need to be building. In the Great Commission, Jesus said, *"Go and make disciples of all nations..."* As the corporate Body of Christ in the earth, is this really our number one priority or are we more inwardly focused or at best are focused outward on a ten- block radius?

The Early Church

I found that the pattern of repentance, faith, obedience, unity and releasing is not just found in the Biblical models discussed thus far. It is a pattern pervasive throughout Scripture both in the Old and New Testaments.

Peter

When Jesus first met Peter, He stepped out onto His boat and told him to push off a bit from the shore. At the direction of the Lord, He told him to let down his nets for a catch. Peter did, even though they had been fishing all night and caught nothing. As he pulled the nets in, there were so many fish that the nets began to tear. He called over to his partners to help and as they assisted him with this massive catch, both of the boats began to sink.

Peter fell on his face before Jesus and said, "...depart from me for I am a wicked man." Jesus replied with, "Come follow me and I will make you a fisher of men." He left his nets and followed him. Right at the start of their relationship, Peter repented, had faith in God, and obeyed the call on his life as Jesus had shared it with him.

Over the course of the next three years, as he ran hard after God, Peter had others join him and was brought into relationship as part of the three, the twelve and the 120. The unity was present throughout the itinerant ministry of Jesus and His disciples as they traveled the countryside.

Jerusalem

The unity piece culminated in the upper room in Jerusalem after Jesus ascended into heaven. As they received power from the Holy Spirit, they went forth and released the deposit that had been placed in them. That first day of the early church at Pentecost, 3,000 were added to their number, which means they began their journey of turning from their sin and their old patterns and turning with faith to God, thus repeating the process.

As the church grew, we see how they lived together. It is recorded, the incredible fellowship of the believers.

> *They devoted themselves to the apostles' teaching and to fellowship, to the breaking of bread and to prayer. Everyone was filled with awe at the many wonders and signs performed by the apostles. All the believers were together and had everything in common. They sold property and possessions to give to anyone who had need. Every day they continued to meet together in the temple courts. They broke bread in their homes and ate with glad and sincere hearts, praising God and enjoying the favor of all the people. And the Lord added to their number daily those who were being saved.*
>
> **Acts 2:42-47**

One thing the Acts 2 church was known for almost above all else, was their unity. The fellowship was so great that they met daily not only in the temple courts, but also in their homes. They cared for one another to such an extent that in Acts 4 it says that there were no poor among them. With this beautiful unity, the Lord added to them daily those who were being saved. Another way of saying that is "...and the Lord added to their number daily those who were coming into repentance and faith."

And thus the process perpetuated. Repentance and faith happened as more were saved each day. Obedience was ongoing as they lived the way that Jesus taught them, caring for each other, loving one another and feeding the poor. Unity was great as their numbers grew and releasing happened as they broke bread together and fed the poor daily (Acts 6). Additionally, the apostles released the deposit that had been placed in them through the wonders and signs that they performed and through their teaching. Others released through the giving to one another and having everything in common.

And so these five things that we saw in the Old Testament on many occasions, the way God was teaching them to live, was the pattern for the perpetuation of the early church and the Gospel message. It was true discipleship, a combination of demonstration and teaching that became a sustainable movement even after the founder of it (Jesus) had returned to heaven. It continued well after the first generation of followers had passed on as well. When persecution struck later in Acts and the Jerusalem church was scattered as those who had been there on the day of Pentecost went home, the model spread and churches sprang up in other locations.

Practical Grace

There are unique characteristics of the Acts 2 church that have many today still studying the model that was birthed through Peter after the upper room experience. The characteristics of fellowship, teaching, breaking of bread and prayer, are prevalent and widespread in most church models that we see in some form today.

Unfortunately, in many places, that is where the similarities stop. We don't find many places in the modern church, particularly in the modern church in America where people are filled with awe at the many signs and wonders that are performed there. The power of Pentecost and the miracles that accompanied the early church are not common anymore.

The idea of selling property and possessions and giving to everyone that had need is something that tends not to even fit in our culture in any way. First of all, in order to sell something and have money left over to give, one would have to be debt-free or nearly debt free. The Acts 2 model is a model of cashing in on inherent equity in real estate and hard assets and utilizing the resulting liquidation as a means of serving those around them in need; a deep expression of extravagant love and grace.

There are many ways to express grace such as healing and forgiveness. Doubt can enter the mind of those who have been healed or forgiven that can rob them of the experience and thus the feeling of redemptive grace. The physical act of paying off a debt or giving resources to someone that has need so closely resembles what Jesus did for us on the cross that it is arguably the best expression of practical grace there is.

After a debt has been paid, a person will not struggle to pay it again.

No one will continue to send payments to a debtor who has declared a debt paid in full. In the same way, if a financial need is provided, the person it was provided for will no longer struggle to meet it. And so, once it's done, it's done.

The act of Jesus dying on the cross for us as the sacrificial lamb means that our debt of sin and death has been paid. A blank check was written that covers all that we've ever done or will ever do. Imagine coming to the realization that your needs are truly met outside of you and without your struggling for that to happen.

Uncommon Love

The love that is expressed through giving of that magnitude is no doubt one of the main attractions to those who were added daily. To be part of a community that took such care of one another, that shared such glad and sincere love for each other that they ate together everyday and would rather sell their own possessions if any among them had need: that is extravagant and uncommon love!

These three things, money, power and love, are some of the most powerful draws to the early church. Apart from each other, they do not have the same meaning. However, putting them together in this incredible combination, they resulted in explosive growth! What church do you know today that started in one day with 120 and had 3,000 more at the end of their first day? And how about adding to their number daily those who were being saved and beginning the path of discipleship? Very uncommon indeed!

Kingdom Culture

*The disciples came to him and asked, "Why do you
speak to the people in parables?" He replied,
"Because the knowledge of the secrets of the
kingdom of heaven has been given to you, but not to
them. Whoever has will be given more, and they will
have an abundance. Whoever does not have, even
what they have will be taken from them."*

Matthew 13:10-12

There is a church that occupies a large warehouse. As you walk in, you
notice right away that this is not a typical church. In fact it is like no
other place you have ever been. There is a lot going on in different
parts of the building. The first thing one notices is the huge table, right
in the middle of the large, open room. It looks like a dining table that
would be in the hall of a king. It is nothing fancy, just really big and
long and has a lot of people at it.

A nice guy named Joel greets you at the door and asks if you are
hungry. You are led over to a seat at the table where you see this
massive spread of food and lots of hungry people eating. It's like one
big family. People are there with little children, some with teenagers,
some older couples and others by themselves. The table has turkey,
mashed potatoes, stuffing, gravy, dinner rolls, salad, green beans and
more.

A little overwhelmed, you sit down and begin to enjoy the food. You observe a man across from you who looks a little rough. He is obviously very hungry. You watch as he grabs a couple of rolls and stuffs them in the inside pocket of his worn coat. A lady, walking by, observes the same thing and smiles at you. She approaches the man and points to a table full of boxes across the room.

"We have lots of food, so feel free to take a box with you. Actually take two if you need it. In fact, we have a truck, we can follow you to your house and load your shelves with all you need." She tells him.

After you are finished eating, you begin to walk around. You see a group praying for some people. There is a large crowd hovering around, some waiting, some crying, some praying and many watching. As you observe for several minutes, you see a lady healed of a life-threatening illness. People are pressing in to see what is happening and the lines are getting longer as word spreads about the lady who was just healed. People are set free from addictions, healed from disease and sickness, and all are standing in awe at what is happening.

At another corner of the room, there is a group gathered around a person teaching. Those listening are intently engaged in the words and concepts being shared. They are studying with the speaker and taking copious notes. Back up near the front, a woman comes in with several children. She is greeted at the door and asked if she needs anything. She begins to explain how her electricity is going to be shut off later this week because she hasn't been making enough money since she lost one of her three jobs.

She is obviously flustered and you can see the desperation in her face as she begins to share her story about her divorce and the struggles raising three little ones on her own. The lady she is pouring her heart out to, puts her arm around her and leads her over to a chair to sit down. "I would be happy to listen to anything you want to share, and we will pray with you and help you, but just tell us your needs right now." she says to her.

The single mom shares about the electric bill and asks if there is any way at all that they can help. The lady helping her brings over a man that takes down some basic information and says they will get right back to her. In the meantime, they take her and the children over to the table and sit them down so they can eat. Right about the time they are finished eating they have her pull her car around and they load it up with boxes of groceries. One of the guys loading the groceries, notice the car is running pretty rough and asks her if it's ok for them to take a look at it. She says sure, so he takes it to the back of the building where there is apparently a car shop.

As the woman comes back in the building, she still has her friend with her, the lady that she initially confided in. The woman needed prayer for some things so she took her up to the prayer area and had several others join with her as they prayed and poured into her. When she is done being prayed for, her new friend takes her over to a group of people sitting at the far wall with computers.

"This is our Human Resource department," she tells her, "We would like to see if we can help you with the right job."

As hope rises in the woman's eyes, she is interviewed by one of the HR people. They ask her about her job skills and past employment and actually put a resume together for her right there. Afterwards, the HR person hands her a list of five different potential places that she can call that are looking for people with her skills.

"How can you do this?" the woman asks.

"We are networked with all the businesses who help us here, so we know their needs." the HR lady responds.

Before she leaves the HR department, she is asked what she really wants to do. Her head dips a little and she related the story of how she was in nursing school years ago when she got pregnant.

"I gave up those dreams long ago." she exclaimed with sadness in her voice.

The HR lady, not deterred by her sadness, responded, "Oh, you have the gift of healing. Come with me."

She leads her over to where people are being prayed for and getting healed. One of the people praying grabs her hand and tells her to hold it out towards the person they are praying for. Several moments later, the one being prayed for looks up and says she is feeling better. As they continue to pray, both the woman praying and the one being prayed for grow in their excitement as the illness the woman had leaves her.

When they are done praying the two women hug and cry together, completely overwhelmed by the experience they have just shared. They exchange numbers so they can meet for coffee and talk more. On her way out, the single mom had forgotten about her electric bill when one of the accountants came up to her and told her, "It's taken care of."

"What is?" she replied a bit taken back.

"Well," the man began, "we paid off your electric bill, your gas bill and your water. We also wiped out your credit card debt and your car payment too. Your rent has been paid three months in advance and you have a car full of groceries. By the way, we tuned up your car and put in new brakes and it's ready to go as well." he responded. "Oh and please let us know if there is anything else we can help you with."

The lady breaks down and begins to sob. Her friend that she had made when she walked in the door holds her and tells her, "...we just want you to know how much God loves you and cares for you."

The single mom accepts Christ and leaves a half hour later. Her life is changed. She is transformed. She walked in heavily burdened with so much stress, loneliness and guilt that she just didn't know where to go. A friend had told her to go to this place where she might find help and so she came as a last resort.

Where?

Whenever I share this story, I am asked, "Where is THAT church?" Everyone wants to know where it is and they all want to go. Why? What is it about that church that's different from all the other churches we go to in America? For one thing, that church is open seven days a week just as described. Secondly, parking is horrendous because there are so many people coming every day that it is hard to handle all the traffic. Yes, it's a real church, it really exists and the address to it is Acts 2:42-47!

They devoted themselves to the apostles' teaching and to fellowship, to the breaking of bread and to prayer. Everyone was filled with awe at the many wonders and signs performed by the apostles. All the believers were together and had everything in common. They sold property and possessions to give to anyone who had need. Every day they continued to meet together in the temple courts. They broke bread in their homes and ate with glad and sincere hearts, praising God and enjoying the favor of all the people. And the Lord added to their number daily those who were being saved.

Acts 2:42-47

This is simply a modern-day model of what they experienced in the "Acts 2 church". Meeting the needs of people wasn't some fuzzy idea; it was real, practical love expressing itself daily. Grace was administered through demonstration. People were loved, cared for and given grace, daily.

Church Today

Why isn't this the norm today? There are three things that are different in this model that we briefly touched on in the last chapter -- money, power and love. We have the teaching and fellowship in just about every expression of church from online church to home churches and everything in between. Prayer is pretty common as well. Breaking of bread happens in a lot of places, too, at least among the good friends in the church it does. What about new people? Are they given the opportunity to break bread with others, or only after they come for a while and get to know some people they can go to Starbuck's with after church? So now begins the departure.

We made it through most of the first sentence describing the early church before there was too much variance with the models we have today. In line 2, though, things get really radical! How many churches are filled with awe at the signs and wonders performed there? In fact, where is a place you know you could take your mom or your sister if she was dying of cancer and have an expectation that she would be healed? Where would you take a drug addict and expect him to be delivered? Where is there POWER?

Some churches do have power. I know of several. I spent some time at one that had healing rooms every week and it was almost commonplace that healings took place. It wasn't taken for granted, but in many of their services, people were asked if they needed healing, and many were healed throughout the services. It was incredible and there was a sense of reverence and awe both in the worship services and the healing times. Unfortunately, this is not the case in many churches I've seen.

For some, a major departure from the early church model and what they experience today occurred in the discussion on power. Those still left tend to check out when we talk about believers having everything in common and selling their property and possessions to give to everyone that had need. Some do not believe this model is right, saying it is an expression of some form of socialism or communism. Others think it is not fair that those who work hard should give to those who aren't working. What about accountability so this system of giving is not taken advantage of? I've heard all of these objections.

To me, there is a root cause for these sincere concerns. The fact is most of our churches are broke. Many of them have debt and those that don't, typically spend all they have in any given year. Beyond that, many of the members live paycheck to paycheck and the average family is so burdened with debt the only thing we could have in common is for you to pay my debt and I'll pay yours. I wonder if this is what Jesus meant by serving money?

Excuses are plentiful when there is either an abundance of lack or an abundance of the perception of lack. Their perception of lack is what we call the "poverty mindset" and it is pervasive in every aspect of life today including the church. Let me ask one question; if a church was debt free with $25 million in cash on deposit and its members were debt free as well, do you think many of the arguments surrounding the perception of lack go away? I do!

Most Christians agree that there is no lack in the Kingdom of God, and yet most agree that there is lack, serious lack, in our churches today. So where is the disconnect? The easy answer is; if there is no lack in the kingdom and there is lack in the church, the church is not in the kingdom, or better said, is not operating in the culture of the kingdom.

Kingdom

There is a big difference between being saved and being in the kingdom; from doing good work and doing kingdom work; from church culture and kingdom culture. Let me ask you this; what caused the undoubted and radical transformation in the life of the single mom in our story above? It was the exact same thing that caused radical transformation in the life of Peter when he met Jesus. Their lives came on a collision course with the kingdom. When confronted with the realities of power, resources, love and grace in the culture of the kingdom, they were radically and irreversibly transformed!

Just like in the life of Peter, the steps of repentance, faith, obedience, unity and releasing all happened to the woman in our story. They also happened on a daily basis in the early church. The life of Jesus is full of these collision points with average people whose lives were forever altered and changed. When He preached, He would say things like, "Repent, for the kingdom of heaven is near." An average life incident upon the kingdom of heaven will be transformed in a powerful way.

You see, Jesus was not about making converts. What He really wanted was disciples, people who would do what He did, people who would demonstrate and teach the good news of the kingdom. It just so happens that making disciples consists of a process of repentance, faith, obedience, unity and releasing. Jesus would teach them about the kingdom and demonstrate it through many miracles of healing the sick, raising the dead, casting out demons and supernaturally manifesting resources such as the water into wine, the fish in the nets (both times), feeding the 5,000+, feeding the 4,000+ and others. He not only taught,

He demonstrated the concept of no lack in the kingdom. That was the good news that He came to preach!

So what is the kingdom then? That is THE question. Throughout the Old Testament, God allowed discipline like recession to align the Israelites, His people. He was after particular things that allowed them to be in alignment and relationship, partnership, if you will, with Him. God ruled His people. When the kings failed, sometimes He used exile to bring them back to repentance, faith, obedience, unity and releasing in the direction of His will for them. Israel was a theocracy, ruled by God. A country ruled by God is in the kingdom of God.

This is why we see the same patterns in the New Testament. God is aligning His people, inviting them to be part of His kingdom. The process of making disciples is the process of alignment with the kingdom. Jesus didn't come to make decision makers, and He didn't call us to do it either. Salvation is part of repentance and faith, but it is only the very beginning of the journey. Once someone has been shown the kingdom and comes into these first two steps, the question becomes, how shall we then live? The way we live is in the kingdom, a different set of patterns.

A pattern or set of patterns of living amongst a group of people is called a culture. We are called to a completely different culture altogether, where we no longer conform to the pattern of this world, but to a different set of principles and values. We learn the patterns of the kingdom. It was what Jesus spent His ministry teaching and demonstrating. It was the good news that He brought to the poor.

There is a different way to live, an alternative culture to live in, called kingdom culture. It's what He created around Him while He was here on earth.

Culture Birthed

The model of church in Acts 2 is one that bears much study. Many books have been written about how we get back to that model. But it wasn't the early church in and of itself that was so special. It was the culture surrounding it. You see, the Acts 2 church was birthed in the culture of the kingdom, the culture that Jesus taught and lived, demonstrating it wherever He went and replicating it through His disciples.

The early church was launched in the environment of kingdom culture. Abundance, healing, life, love, grace, power, resources all flowed out of or were released through the church because it was operating in the kingdom. Church is who we are, while kingdom is what we create and how we live. It should be the culture surrounding the church. That's how it was designed to work.

Church without the culture of the kingdom doesn't have the punch. It lacks the power, the draw, the resources and the love. Quite frankly, it's religion. It's a form of godliness that denies the power. When we operate in the fullness of this culture, we experience the fullness of the kingdom. Each individual is connected in unity, flowing in their gift and calling, living out their destiny with abundant provision. The supernatural is an outgrowth of the culture that flows in the kingdom.

Some churches flow in love, they really get that, and some lives are changed with that love. Some churches flow in healing and many are brought to salvation and healed through that culture. A few churches operate at the level of abundant provision that we see in the early church. I believe we can operate in one aspect of kingdom culture and negate other aspects by what we teach, believe and demonstrate.

We, the church, are designed to operate in all aspects of kingdom culture. We are designed to live our vizion through a community of like-minded brothers and sisters that love us and are committed to pursuing the call of God on their own life and the lives of all connected. They are actively pursuing the discipling of nations, which, again, is part of their culture. Kingdom is sustainable. It's reciprocal and perpetuating. It happens organically on every level and in all aspects of life.

Separation of church and state was designed to limit the occupation of one super power voice of God acting as His personal governance on the earth. The church is designed to provide the moral value system or culture that society is governed by on all seven mountains of influence or aspects of life. It is not designed to control governments on every level. In kingdom culture, the principles of the kingdom invade every level of society setting up His kingdom on the earth. No one particular church or person controls it all but the culture is pervasive through the Lordship of Jesus in the lives of all peoples on all levels. This is what discipling nations means, to perpetuate and replicate kingdom cultures to all tribes, tongues, nations and peoples.

The first request in the Lord's Prayer is that "your kingdom come and your will be done on earth as it is in heaven..." He was praying to God the Father and thus His kingdom is the Kingdom of God. His request that it would be on earth as in heaven, which means the kingdom of heaven, is the kingdom of God and when Jesus came down to earth, He brought the kingdom with Him. That is why He says numerous times, ***"Repent, for the kingdom of heaven is near (or at hand)."*** It was near because Jesus was here establishing Kingdom culture on the earth.

Financial WAR!

From the days of John the Baptist until now the
kingdom of heaven suffers violence, and violent men
take it by force.

Matthew 11:12 (NIV)

The most powerful lies are those that contain 99% truth. Somewhere along the way, we bought the lie. It is evident in our churches, our families, our budgets, our outreach programs, our careers and our lives. When did the cause become a hobby? When did the Great Commission become optional? When did living our God-ordained purpose become a choice? When did we decide that the ultimate goal was to spend the largest portion of our lives working for our own comfort and happiness? Where is the passion? Where is the legacy?

Providing for your family is not a bad thing, in fact, it's a good thing, it just cannot be the main thing. Obedience to God needs to be and we cannot abdicate our responsibility to His destiny for us any longer on the altar of "financial security." God provided for the legacy and future of the Israelites when they came out of Egypt, but the plunder was not just for their families, it was to build the tabernacle. As they laid down their treasure for the vizion that God had, He provided them the Promised Land, a land of their own, flowing with milk and honey.

In Haggai, God provided for them to go back to Jerusalem to rebuild the temple and showered them with prosperity while they were there, but when building homes for themselves and their families became the main thing ahead of building a house for Him to dwell, He withheld the resources from them to align them to the task He called them to. Once they were aligned and on task with what He called them to do, God brought prosperity and blessing back to them and in abundance!

In Nehemiah, the people could not provide for their families because of the economic environment. They were having trouble just surviving! Many had to go into debt to feed their families, mortgaging their homes, fields and vineyards. In some cases, they had to sell their children into slavery to ensure they were cared for. In the midst of such dire circumstances, as they were obedient to rebuild the wall, God set them free from the debt and slavery by canceling their principal balances and having the interest paid back to them in full.

There is absolutely NOTHING Biblical about a model that perpetuates the lie that the goal of money is to make me comfortable and ensure my wealth doesn't run out before I die. NOTHING! Can I say it again, N-O-T-H-I-N-G!!! Our financial life, as a Christian should never be about financial "peace". Financial peace implies the absence of worry. That somehow, through careful planning and diligent, meticulous budgeting we can insulate ourselves from every worry that is caused by a life run by money. Peace, however, is not the absence of worry but the presence of trust. Thus true peace can ONLY be obtained by trusting in an omnipotent God who rescues, resources and sends us to do His work. Our peace comes from knowing that we are God's and that He will provide all our needs financial or otherwise. He and He alone is our source. HE ALONE!

The concept of financial peace to many is a comfortable, peaceful, co-existence with money where we have agreed on terms to cohabitate. I will work hard and save a lot and then I can live like no one else. It equates to sleeping with the enemy. Comfort with your financial position and worse yet, working to achieve that comfort will cause us not to take risks, not to reach out for the unknown and ultimately not to trust God. Budgets and planning are good tools, as is money, designed to serve us and the purpose for which we were made. Financial responsibility, as we have presented here, is part of faithfulness to God and to the call on our lives. It is a component of obedience to step out and do what He called us to do. But make no mistake, if our vizion leads to where our budget cannot, in the pattern of the kingdom, money serves us, not us it!

What we need is financial WAR! Money is not just a tool, it is a weapon, to violently advance the Kingdom of God! Period! That's what it's for. When we've lost sight of who we are, and begin to think life is about us, it becomes easy to cozy up to our friend – money. After all, God wants me blessed, right? He wants me to prosper...

> *No one can serve two masters; for either he will hate the one and love the other, or he will be devoted to one and DESPISE the other. You can't serve both God and money.*
>
> **Matthew 6:24 (NASB)**

These are the words of Jesus Himself. Why don't we preach on the hatred of money in our churches then? Why don't we despise it to the level that we only want to keep the minimum that we need to live on and give the rest away, far from us? Why don't we take these words seriously? Money is our slave, like the sword in the hand of a seasoned warrior. It helps us accomplish the purpose of our lives, like the sword is an extension of the arm of a soldier.

Why can't most Americans walk away from their jobs today and head to the mission field? Why? It is because of debt. To be a missionary in most mission agencies, you need to be debt free. Why? It is considered financially irresponsible to raise support from others that is used to pay off your debt! And so, if we can't leave our jobs, because of debt and our lifestyle, who are we serving in that lifestyle? Is it God or money?

Is saving bad? Not at all. Is getting out of debt bad? No, it's almost always a good thing, unless either of them prevent us from stepping out to accomplish the vizion for our lives. Financial security or financial peace speak to a feeling of safety centered in serving or properly handling an inanimate object. Remember, in Haggai, they felt safe. They were prosperous enough to build paneled houses of royal design; and yet they had forsaken the calling and the purpose of their prosperity. God dried up the resources they enjoyed to align them with His will. It is possible, that we can do everything "right" financially by the world's standards, have a great job, be debt-free and save a pile of money. If we are not aligned with God's will for our lives, we should expect those resources and that security to be blown away quickly.

Some feel that they can give their way to prosperity as well. The Bible clearly states that "obedience is better than sacrifice." It's interesting in Joel, God even dried up the sacrifices! God can and will, according to the Biblical models, dry up or blow away even your ability to give in order to align you in obedience to what He has called you to do!

> *Grain offerings and drink offerings are cut off from the house of the LORD. The priests are in mourning, those who minister before the LORD. Put on sackcloth, you priests, and mourn; wail, you who minister before the altar. Come, spend the night in sackcloth, you who minister before my God; for the grain offerings and drink offerings are withheld from the house of your God.*
>
> **Joel 1:9, 13**

Comfort can come in many forms: not just money itself, but financial security. Sometimes I wonder if portions of the 'marketplace ministry movement' haven't inadvertently become a way to make those who are slaves to money and thus their jobs, feel better about where they are. "God has called me to business..." But has He really? What disciple stayed involved in the marketplace after Jesus called Him? Did Jesus stay a carpenter after He was led into ministry? Surely the Lord can use the marketplace as a way to reach people like Jesus did but that doesn't mean God has called you to a job you hate so you can invite a few people to church. If it's your mission field, awesome! Treat is as such. But if it's not, get in obedience to what He has called you to do! Trust Him to provide as you step out.

So is it that God has called us to be 'marketplace ministers' or simply that we are serving money and can't leave? OUCH! How much of what we do in the church world is built on false foundations, particularly in the areas of finance?!?! It is interesting to me the number of people that I talk to who feel they are "called" to the marketplace and yet their plan is for God to bless them with millions so they can quit and go do missions. I have a question, if God called you to marketplace ministry, why would that change once you had incredible wealth and resources to do something else?

Here are the facts:

1) We are ALL called to the Great Commission, to GO and make DISCIPLES of ALL nations.

2) We each have a vizion, purpose or calling that fits directly into the corporate call to GO and make disciples of all nations.

3) Most of us, if we inherited a pile of money, or won the lottery, would quit what we are doing today and pursue something else entirely; something more along the lines of our dreams and passions.

Why? Why don't we do that thing now? Why don't we quit our jobs, pursue the destiny and the dream that God placed inside our hearts and trust Him to provide? It's simple really, and yet, here we are, working every day, day in and day out; most of us having marginal, if any, impact on the work environment, our companies and our colleagues.

When I was working in management at a Fortune 500 company, I felt called to the paychecks every two weeks, and honestly, I would probably still be there if God had not ousted me, by His incredible grace and favor! I love what I do now. He freed me! Rescued me, resourced me and sent me on a vizion that I am passionate about. He made me not a missionary, but a vizionary. I work in the marketplace but it is truly ministry and I know how my calling fits into His plan for the world, the Great Commission.

Tell me you're not serving money, please! Tell me the reason you are staying where you are is the intense burning desire and passion you have for your co-workers where you weep over them daily that God would tarry and use you to bring them to salvation. I pray this is true for all of us! It sure wasn't for me!

Can God use us where we are? Absolutely! But let's be real; how many of us feel really called to the jobs that we have, so called that if we suddenly came into a $10M fortune, we would stay in our current position and continue working? Our "ministry" there is so valuable to us and the core of just who we are that they could not pay us enough to leave. Where is our calling, where is our conviction, where is the war for us? What mountain are we willing to die on, what hill are we called to take that we would sacrifice all at great personal risk to see His kingdom established?

People serve money out of a lack of faith. It takes guts to step out into the promise God has for us, it takes risk to go after our dream. It's scary, it's uncomfortable, it takes great courage, an iron spine, incredible faith and obedience; its almost, like warfare.

For us to be the best, our best, we need to be actively pursuing what God made us for. When we're not, we die a little each day; a slow painful death! Our dream dies too and suddenly we become a prisoner in our own lies. This is what conformity looks like! We find ourselves saying things like, "I can't leave my job and go after my dream, that is irresponsible! What about my family? What about my lifestyle? What about my retirement and my future with the company? What about my seniority?" Are these just excuses holding us back, positioning us firmly on the sidelines, out of the battle and feeling "safe"? Not that we are safe, we just feel that way for the time being. Until the stock market crashes, until there is corporate downsizing, until crisis, and then what? Then we find life very uncomfortable, and we have a hard time trusting God because we never did it before, not on this level!

I felt this way with a long military career until things changed and I left the military. I found security in a publicly traded company in a management position, until the company was investigated by several states' Attorneys General and they started firing entire regions of people. I left there before I got the ax. I worked for a Fortune 500 Company in management as well. My average colleague worked there 20 years and most of us were looking at retiring there. That job lasted 5 months before the government shut down the nuclear power plant I worked at. A ton of us lost our jobs on that one. And so I found myself in the mortgage business. I was doing well there and at my peak and the peak of the market, when I felt the call of God to go do something else. I left the security of that position for a life of uncertainly and an incredible journey and adventure with God.

Not Safety - Exile

You see, we weren't safe, anymore than the Israelites were in Egypt. We were in exile. We were slaves to money. We served a wicked master that is never satisfied, that never has enough that never quits and never lets up; conforming to the pattern of this world. Why is it that so many people, several years after they were fired or let go, are happier than they have ever been? Because they were rescued! They had no option but to go do something else and so they finally chose to do that thing they loved, the thing that always drove them, what they always wanted to do. What would the world be like if we all did that thing NOW?

When we're not in our purpose and destiny, the world lacks our piece. The body of Christ lacks our input and the Great Commission lacks our part. So let's just stop pretending that God's will is for us is to stay in a dead end job, so He can "use" us there, ok? Please? He wants us free, at our best, living a life of adventure, the one we were designed to live, trusting Him and violently advancing the kingdom! When we are in our purpose, we are SO much more passionate, more engaged and more deadly to the enemy than at any other time in our lives. We are downright dangerous to the kingdom of darkness!

Weapons

Money is a weapon, a tool, designed to serve us, like an ornate broad sword; the kind that William Wallace used in the movie 'Brave heart'. Or think of the sword that Conan wields in the original movies. It is the sword in 'Lord of the Rings' that was broken but has been remade. It is a symbol of the family. It bears the crest and the name and is an invaluable part of the clan's heritage and legacy.

But imagine a sword such as these, carefully placed in its sheath and hidden in the family vault, safe, protected, secure. It is well polished, without stain or blemish and carefully preserved. Why? Is it so that we may hand it down to the next generation who will carefully preserve it as a symbol? Is it a symbol of all our ancestors fought for; of days gone by and battles won and lost? Is it a symbol of the legacy we leave to our children and our children's children?

To some, that is all that money is. It's just a symbol. It has little meaning except status or comfort. It is carefully earned, painstakingly protected and polished and stored away for safe keeping. Why? Is it so they have something to pass on to their children? A legacy? My brothers, sisters and fellow warriors, that is a legacy of impotence, a legacy for cowardice. It is a legacy of one that failed to risk and fight, one that did not face the challenges of the day. It was a sword protected, not one that was wielded. No battles were won, no foes defeated. Its blade never tasted the blood of an enemy, never the clash against another.

And so protected, it was passed down to the next generation, - with a legacy of impotence, a family history of cowardice. It will teach our children never to risk greatness for God, never to expend themselves on behalf of the kingdom. Instead, go to college, get a job, make a good living and save for retirement. The sword is passed but the legacy becomes embedded, the legacy of fear, doubt, and paralysis. Play it safe, my son, don't take risks.

Be conformed to the pattern of this world. Get up, go to work, come home and go to bed for about 45 years and then hit a white ball around a grassy knoll and call it living.

Once we step out into what He's called us to and taste of the adventure and His incredible provision in that adventure, we will never look back! We won't be held a slave to money anymore. We will truly be free. Financial freedom is not enough money to never worry, it IS the trust in God that will never allow a situation, in spite of how dire it appears, to rob us of our trust in Him and the resolve to push on. Yes, there were comforts in Egypt that they didn't have in the desert. Yes, it was hot and the road was long, but the physical presence of the Lord God Almighty was with them wherever they went. Yes, there will be giants in our promised land, but when we remember it's not about us, and not by our might, they will lie defeated at our feet.

There is a peace in the realm of battle that is most honorable. It's the peace that comes when faced with the enemy, when surrounded on all sides; our mind becomes fixed, our gaze lifted to the horizon, above the fray, over the heads of the advancing giants to the light beyond. This is peace when at the moment of certain death or defeat we can resign ourselves to move forward in the destiny we were created for and to die trying rather than retreating. This is the moment in which we know the calling and the purpose that lies before us and we are committed to the path that will take us through it or wreck all ability to ever recover. Our trust is in God, and come what may, our courage will not fail! With a fixed mind and a steadfast heart we run forward, into the battle!

Armies

Imagine a church where everyone in it was empowered and encouraged to take the risk and live their dreams, not someday, but TODAY! Imagine how we could network and come together assisting each other in the call on our lives with the gifts and talents each had to bring to the table, releasing our talents and resources to each other, working together as a force. What would such a church of just 50 people look like? What about 100? What about 500 or 1,000 people all moving forward in the destiny and purpose to which God called us, in unity, running hard after Him without fear, without trepidation, without pause. It could look like the last major battle scene in the 'Return of the King' film (third in the Lord of the Rings trilogy), where there is a small band of brothers, hardened warriors who had risked it all in support of one. They are completely surrounded by a massive army that totally dwarfs them and yet they charge out to meet them.

Their leader rides out in front of them and calls out,

> *"My brothers, I see in your eyes the same fear that would take the heart of me. A day may come when the courage of men fails, when we forsake our friends and break all bonds of fellowship, but it is not THIS day, an hour of wolves and shattered shields when the age of men comes crashing down but it is not this day, THIS day we fight!"*

Could 100 people, completely sold out, leave behind comfort and safety, venture into the vast unknown with God, partner with Him and live their purpose and destiny? Could not a group like this, a band of warriors and princess warriors turn around a city? Could not transformation be wrought through a group such as these who dared to meet the challenge of their calling head on? Would not the world be a different place?

And now imagine that times 10,000! What if, 10,000 churches of any size stood up and said we will fight for the soul of this nation. We will fight for the marriages, families, children, prostitutes, drug addicted, homeless and lost. We will risk comfort and security and live out our purpose and destiny in the face of certain danger. We will dare to live the life we are called and for the purposes we are designed. We will step out, abandoning the patterns of this world and combine our lives, our sacred honors and our fortunes for the dream that is on God's heart. Reckless abandon to retirement plans, comfortable living, status quo and security. We will use the talents and abilities God gave us, the resources we have, ALL of them and our abilities to create wealth to violently pursue the lost, to take ground for God, to advance His kingdom and make His name great in the earth! Let us be numbered among those who risked it all, who rode out to meet the challenge and who left a legacy for generations to come!

Legacy

Imagine the legacy for our children. There are swords bloodied by battle, dinged up by the clash of steel against steel, but there is a legacy of trust and faith in God, unafraid to risk it all. Swords that were drawn and used, battles that were fought side-by-side with our kids as we prayed for God's provision and moved forward in His destiny for our families together, all part of the legacy and a history of the faithfulness of God, written down and remembered for generations. There are stories of battles fought with our children watching our every move and learning with us to hear the voice of our God saying, "This is the way, walk in it."

Will that be you? Will it start with you in your church, in your community, in your family? Instead of being the first to go to college, be the first to risk it all and follow your dream, the dream of God for your life. Who will stand up and be numbered? Who will no longer conform? Who will lead the charge and create around them a cadre of like-minded warriors who will advance with you? Will you be the leader to start transformation in your city? Will you be counted among those who lived the adventure, trusted God, and risked it?

Is this not an awesome picture of kingdom culture? Would our efforts not disciple our children, our communities and ultimately nations? Let's do it, together. Let's partner and work to bring the resources, training and tools needed to start the revolution in our world. Let's care about the things that break the heart of God together. Let's forcefully advance the kingdom together and watch what God does!

> *But seek first His kingdom and His righteousness*
> *and all these things will be added unto you."*
>
> **Matthew 6:33**

Occupy, Church

The LORD said to me, "See, I have begun to deliver Sihon and his land over to you. Begin to occupy, that you may possess his land."

Deuteronomy 2:31 (NASB)

As the Israelites wandered in the desert after the Exodus out of Egypt, God led them into the land of Heshbon where Sihon was king. God told Moses that he had given him into his hand so that they may possess the land. Sihon and all his people came out to meet the Israelites in battle and they were defeated, giving Israel the land of Heshbon.

What happens during and after a war is called an occupation. An advancing army overtakes a defense force, capturing them as slaves or killing them off. The war we are engaged in is not a physical war of one army against another. It is a spiritual war fought with spiritual weapons with lives hanging in the balance. This war is not just fought on spiritual grounds but also through culture and influence; for culture captivates and often rules the hearts and minds of men. So how do we "occupy" in a spiritual war in the physical realm?

Sometime ago, God released a strategy regarding the transformation of an entire culture by a relatively small group of people. The idea is that if the experts or authorities at the top of seven spheres or categories of influence (often called the seven mountains) are in agreement or unity, they can turn the tide of culture and thus the direction of the nation.

These seven mountains are business, government, media, arts and entertainment, education, family and religion. A relatively small group of people (1-2% of the whole population) can determine or disciple a nation.

I first heard the story at a "Seven Mountains" Conference that I attended in North Carolina back in 2008. As the story goes, the strategy was given simultaneously to Bill Bright (founder of Campus Crusade for Christ) and Loren Cunningham (founder of Youth with a Mission) the two largest Christian mission organizations in the world. They both felt led to share it with the other and so they met. They both pulled out the notes they had written down, at the same time and swapped them only to find out it was the same strategy!

About a year later, I had the pleasure of working with YWAM (Youth with a Mission) at the University of Nations in Kona, Hawaii with Loren Cunningham. During the week I spent there, I worked closely with Loren on a real estate and finance project and we enjoyed numerous conversations. One evening, we were sitting alone in his minivan and I asked him to tell me the story of the seven mountains strategy. This is what he related to me;

"I was up in the mountains with my family in Colorado. We came in one day and the next morning I just got a download from the Lord and I wrote it out as fast as He gave it to me, in these seven areas. These were the basis, out of which the many subgroups would be born. Every society in the world from the simplest tribal group, has seven of those, they may use drums or smoke signals or something else to shout it from the mountaintops to communicate publicly, but (they have) every one of them.

I got a call from the ranger. There was a call coming in, that Bill and Vonette were in the state and they wanted to see us, since they are our friends. I went and took him the list. He pulled out his list before I did, I was reaching to pull it out, mine was yellow, his was on white paper, and he said, "Look Loren, look what God showed me!"

"This is what God showed me!" I responded. My wife heard Francis Shaeffer on TV three weeks later give the same list; and so we felt God was saying it was not just for YWAM, it was for the entire body of Christ. So that was a huge shift in missions, helping to fulfill chapter 28 of Matthew and discipling all nations. Disciple them in the categories and then the subcategories that Campus Crusade now calls the gateways. In a complex society there are many gateways underneath, so we go in and disciple people in the categories."

The strategy of the seven mountains was a huge shift in missions as Loren stated. Instead of going into a country with an evangelism mindset to just convert people to Christ, as had been done for years, we now have an approach that allows the culture of the kingdom to shift the culture of a nation or people group. This is why culture is so vitally important! It's why transformation, or conforming no longer to the pattern of the world, is critical in aligning us to disciple nations.

Imagine if the influencers in the seven areas were discipled in the culture and the Gospel of the kingdom, could we not turn whole nations to God?

It's interesting to note the disciples and friends that Jesus associated with were from every walk of life and cultural level. He was influencing culture, saturating it with the culture of the kingdom. That was the "good news" that He came to share. Salvation and grace was a part of that, but the good news to the poor that set the captives free was the life that they could live, the very culture of heaven that they have access to.

In September 2011, a movement arose in an attempt to shift culture in America, the Occupy Wall Street movement. Although many varied messages and shameful acts have come out of this movement, this fact remains: Occupy Wall Street, at its roots, is a cry for justice. The Declaration of the Occupation of New York City, the first official document to come out of the Occupy Wall Street movement, contains these words in its opening sentence:

"As we gather together in solidarity to express a feeling of mass injustice, we must not lose sight of what brought us together."

The cry for justice from this generation is not unique to the United States. A similar cry has been raised and heard around the world this past spring and summer. People are longing to throw off the chains of injustice and the oppressed are longing to be free: free from oppression, free from injustice, free from corruption. They are not just longing to be free, but they have taken to the streets to fight for it.

In 2011, in what was dubbed as 'Arab Spring' revolutions occurred forcing rulers from power in Tunisia, Egypt, Libya, and Yemen; civil uprisings erupted in Bahrain and Syria; major protests in Algeria, Iraq, Jordan, Kuwait, Morocco and Oman; and minor protests in Lebanon, Mauritania, Saudi Arabia, Sudan and Western Sahara. Protests in Jordan caused the sacking of two successive governments by King Abdullah.

This is no small thing! What happened in New York and around the world in 2011 is not something to be ignored. It's a generation crying out for justice. Hunger for justice is good! It is not only good, it's Biblical, and we should expect it. We are told that:

> *For the anxious longing of the creation waits eagerly*
> *for the revealing of the sons of God. For the creation*
> *was subjected to futility, not willingly, but because of*
> *Him who subjected it, in hope that the creation itself*
> *also will be set free from its slavery to corruption into*
> *the freedom of the glory of the children of God.*
> **Romans 8:19-21**

Creation longs to be free from slavery to corruption. The cry that came out of Zuccotti Park is exactly that – freedom from corruption! The very idea of the Occupy Wall Street movement began with one simple demand – a Presidential commission to separate money from politics: freedom from slavery to corruption!

Biblical Protest

Is there any Biblical basis for this cause? In another time of recession and mortgage crisis, a group of men and women raised a cry of protest against their fellow countrymen. They were saying, *"We have such large families. We need more money just so we can buy the food we need to survive."* Others said, *"We have mortgaged our fields, businesses, and homes to get food during the recession."* And others said, *"We have already borrowed to the limit on our fields and vineyards to pay our taxes. We belong to the same family, and our children are just like theirs. Yet we must sell our children into slavery just to get enough money to live. We have already sold some of our daughters, and we are helpless to do anything about it, for our fields and vineyards are already mortgaged to others."*

You know what the response of God's chosen leader was? He took care of those hurting and led them out. God used Nehemiah like He used Moses and even Haggai as a leader who led the way back to God. This is exactly the incident that occurred in Nehemiah 5. He also rebuked the nobles and officials who, through greed, were taking advantage of the situation and worsening the hardship for many.

In case you missed this, the actions following the mortgage crisis of 2008 have been exactly opposite of the patterns we have seen. There has been no repentance, and in most cases, not even an admission of guilt! There has been no faith in God, no obedience, no unity and the releasing that happened was the government releasing our tax dollars to the very institutions responsible for the mess we are in! Hence, the country has not recovered, recession has not lifted, things have gradually gotten worse and economists are now saying, we haven't even hit the bottom yet. So, what is the response of the Church to be in this hour? Responses are all over the map currently, almost as varied as the messages coming out of the Wall Street protests. Forget the opinions; disregard the hype, for even many Christian leaders are getting this one wrong. What does God say? What does the Bible say? What is the solution when a cry of freedom from corruption and injustice is heard?

> *Is not this the kind of fasting I have chosen: to loose the chains of injustice and untie the cords of the yoke, to set the oppressed free and break every yoke? Is it not to share your food with the hungry and to provide the poor wanderer with shelter—when you see the naked, to clothe them, and not to turn away from your own flesh and blood? Then your light will break forth like the dawn, and your healing will quickly appear; then your righteousness will go before you, and the glory of the LORD will be your rear guard. Then you will call, and the LORD will answer; you will cry for help, and he will say: Here am I."*

This is God talking to His people: His people – the Church! We declare fasts and pray for the "...*healing of our land...*" we cite 2 Chronicles 7:14 and shout "...*if my people...*" but do we ignore the cries for justice? Are we feeding the poor? Are we providing the wanderer with shelter? Are we clothing the naked? Are we taking care of our own countrymen?!?! Revival doesn't come with prayer and fasting alone! Like with Haggai and Joel, repentance, faith and unity are needed, and yet obedience is critical too. Without obedience and releasing, the recovery is not promised.

People are hurting and looking for answers. Unemployment is at record highs, poverty is on the rise, and people have lost their homes in record numbers. Statistically some cities, like Detroit, look similar to places in the third world. It is the destiny and purpose of the Church to declare the message of grace, love and hope. That message is to feed the hungry, and take care of the poor and oppressed, to demonstrate and teach the Gospel of the Kingdom. It's who we are!

> *If you do away with the yoke of oppression, with the*
> *pointing finger and malicious talk, and if you spend*
> *yourselves in behalf of the hungry and satisfy the*
> *needs of the oppressed,*
> *then your light will rise in the darkness,*
> *and your night will become like the noonday.*
> *The LORD will guide you always;*
> *he will satisfy your needs in a sun-scorched land and*
> *will strengthen your frame.*
> *You will be like a well-watered garden,*
> *like a spring whose waters never fail.*
> *Your people will rebuild the ancient ruins and will*
> *raise up the age-old foundations; you will be called*
> *Repairer of Broken Walls, Restorer of Streets with*

Dwellings.

Isaiah 58:6-12

I found this verse by doing a search on Bible gateway.com for Wall Street in the Bible. Do you think it's interesting that broken walls and streets are both mentioned in the last verse of this passage? Do you find it intriguing that while many in this country want to restore the America the founding fathers had in mind, there is a Biblical way to raise up the age-old foundations?

In a time of economic upheaval, in a time of financial recession, in a time of injustice and corruption; will the Church arise and be the shining light she is called to be? We see clearly in Isaiah 58 how to do it. For such a time as this! Let us rise! Let us be the spring whose waters never fail! Let us be the light breaking forth in this time of darkness. Let's be the light that this generation is crying out for! We need the demonstration, message and culture of the Kingdom!

Potential of Biblical Proportions

Because of the debt loads that we carry as Christians, because of the massive debt on most churches, we don't have flexibility to fund ministry and thus we are not meeting the mandate of Isaiah 58. Only seven cents of every dollar given to a church goes to feed the poor. One half of one cent is spent reaching the unreached people groups or taking the Gospel to nations that have not yet heard.

Because we have not been intentional in following the Lord Almighty's financial and economic plans, we are left in a de facto status where our budgeting methods do not allow us the resources to do what He called us to do. We look at missions and benevolence as optional, outreach dependent on revenue and mortgages and debt the modus operandi in church culture. In a great many cases, we're serving money instead of God and the world around us is hurting because of it! So how can we change?

Financial Releasing

Tithing - literally meaning "a tenth", is the act of giving 10% of your income to the Lord. Many people believe that it is Biblically mandated and that most or all of it should go to the local church. Some believe it is a mandate, others believe it is a guideline. The Bible clearly tells us obedience is better than sacrifice and while a tenth can certainly be used as a Biblical guideline, we find under the principles of releasing that He may call us to give much more.

Here are a couple facts: less than 1 out of 5 people in churches today tithe. With that, the evangelical Christian churches in America bring in a combined $80 Billion a year in gross income. We can estimate from that at least 25% or $20B is spent paying interest on church mortgages.

Why do such a relatively small amount (20%) of people in churches today tithe? This is probably for the same reason the Israelites weren't building elaborate tabernacles in Egypt. They either aren't willing, their hearts have not been moved, or they lack the ability to give. Many people feel like they can't even pay their bills; they are in debt, some have lost their jobs or taken pay cuts and our country has been in an economic recession. It's like asking the Israelites to fund a building project before they were rescued and resourced!

There is a difference between deciding what to do with money you have and giving to a cause, knowing you can't afford it and expecting God to make up the slack. The truth is the average American family has $30,000 in consumer debt. This does not include mortgages! Most of this is credit card debt, student loans and car payments. We are not

> **In 2 years, with all debt gone and the operating budget the same, the church would have more for ministry & outreach than the entire initial budget!**

free from debt as the Israelites were. We need to be rescued and resourced like they were for the original model to work.

What if, like Moses, we could lead the people in the churches out of debt and bondage and show them how to be resourced more than they were before? If people had more of an ability to give, do you think it's possible that the number of people in a given church who tithe could increase from 1 out of 5 to just 2 out of 5? That's only one more person out of every 5, really just a marginal shift, only 20%. If that happens, that church would double its income immediately! A church with a gross income of $2M a year would now have $4M a year without adding one new member. This is an economic model, not a growth model. Imagine this, if that church applied the extra income to pay off mortgage debt, most churches would be completely free of their mortgages in about 2 years! Double income with no debt, talk about abundant resourcing! Here's what that would look like:

Single Church Potential

Gross Income 1 out of 5 people tithing = $2M

$$\$2M - \$500{,}000 \quad\quad = \$1.5M$$
(Gross revenue − mortgage debt   = Operating budget)

Gross Income 2 out of 5 people tithing = $4M

Gross Income − Operating Budget = $2.5M
(Money left over for ministry and outreach)

We talked about what it would mean if just one more person out of every 5 in our churches gave 10% of their income. It would free up more money every year for ministry and outreach and get the church out of debt inside of 2 years! But what if we followed the idea in Nehemiah? What if every person in a church was out of debt? By operating in the culture of the kingdom, we can have an expectation of debt forgiveness, exponential growth and supernatural provision. The average family in America has what we call a 30% debt-to-income ratio, which means that 30% of the income brought into a family is used to pay debt payments.

Individual/Family Monthly Spending

WITH DEBT	OR	**WITHOUT DEBT**
Sample family income = $4,167		Sample family income = $4,167
- Average family debt (30% of income) = $1,250		- *Money for ministry* (30% of income) = **$1,250**
- Average Living Expenses = $2,083		- Average Living Expenses = $2,083
- Tithe = $417		- Tithe = $417
= Discretionary or left-over money = $417		= Discretionary or left-over money = $417

If we were completely out of debt, we would free up this additional 30% of our income. We could use it to fund ministry *without any noticeable change in our lifestyles*. Notice the living expenses, tithe and discretionary monies all stay the same. This money could be used to fund a ministry that the Lord puts on your heart like a missionary, a church or a food bank. Or it could be used to fund the vizion that God has given YOU!

For many people, the first step in truly working towards their vizion is getting out of debt so they have the ability to invest in what the Lord has placed in front of them, the vizion or God-dream that they are called to pursue. I'd also like to point out that time and again, when people put God first, He not only provides seed to the sower but multiplies what they bring in. Their releasing allows more resources to flow to them.

On Earth as it is...

...your kingdom come, your will be done, on earth as it is in heaven...

Matthew 6:10

Jesus prayed that the kingdom of the Father, the kingdom of God, would come on the earth, as it exists in heaven. I often think that I have no grasp of what that really looks like. The kingdom of heaven on this earth would have all the power, all the authority, all the grace, favor, love, resources, provision, peace and joy, all of that here, now, on earth as it is in heaven. The very reason most Christians want to get to heaven is to experience the culture of the kingdom. What if we can have that here and now and still be a part of what God is doing in the earth!

But how do we do this? We understand from Romans 12:2 that we are no longer to be conformed to the pattern of this world, but to be transformed by the renewing of our minds. We also understand that we are to go and disciple nations, which is the Great Commission. But do we see the connection between these two verses? How can we disciple nations if the culture we carry doesn't change? How can the culture we carry change if we are not transformed? How can we be transformed without renewing out minds?

Repentance, thinking differently, begins in the mind. It is brought about and activated in our lives by the Word of God and the presence of God.

Like Peter in the boat upon meeting Jesus and experiencing the monstrous catch of fish; a life incident upon the demonstration of the kingdom of God seeks repentance. The lack in our lives is exposed and the response is change. Faith also, begins with the hearing of the good news of the kingdom. It permeates our being, creating a desire of more, a belief that more is possible and an alignment with the One through which it comes alive.

Obedience is the act of bringing our actions and our lifestyle into alignment with the renewed mind and heart that we have through repentance and faith. It is action, moving forward, living intentionally in the new culture in which we have been accepted. Moving, flowing, walking in the path of the kingdom produces unity with others who are doing the same. Our goals become aligned, our purposes in agreement and our destiny – common. Life is not about us; it is about the kingdom and is shared together with those with whom we walk.

This then is releasing, the flow of gifts, talents, abilities, resources, provision, grace, favor and love, the commodities of the kingdom which are freely given and freely received. Needs are met, resources provided, there is no lack. Vizions, goals, objectives, budgets, systems, plan and accountabilities are all aligned toward the achievement of the common mission as we work together with God and the resources of heaven at hand to accomplish His will, His purpose.

Those around us readily observe this culture, love and unity. Others, not yet in the kingdom but coming in contact with it will have a desire for more. They followed Jesus all through the countryside; they brought the sick, the dying and the dead to Him for healing. They were brought into the culture and began to see the resources of heaven as the solution to the problems in their lives. They only had to reach out and touch it like the woman with the issue of blood. The kingdom of heaven was truly at hand!

So the call falls to us, at this time, in this generation. The call is to not be conformed any longer to the pattern of this world but to be transformed by the renewing of our minds that we may be able to test and approve what His will is, His good, perfect and pleasing will. Go therefore and make disciples of all nations, baptizing them in the name of the Father, the Son and the Holy Spirit and teaching them to obey all that I have commanded you and lo, I will be with you always, even to the very end of the age.

In other words, do not be conformed to the pattern of this world, but be transformed by the renewing of your mind (through repentance, faith, obedience, unity and releasing) and go transform the world. Become an active part of the culture of the kingdom, and share that culture with others. Disciple nations, establish My kingdom here on earth as it is in heaven! Without personal transformation, none of this is possible. Without the culture of heaven permeating our every cell, our lives, everything we do, with resources, power and love, our task is impossible.

What would the kingdom of God on earth look like practically today? For it to be real, it has to be tangible. For it to be tangible, it has to be measurable. Jesus fed the 5,000 men plus women and children with 5 loaves and 2 fishes. They had 12 baskets left over. It was a measurable and tangible miracle of provision. So let's start there.

Is it possible to solve world hunger in one generation, a generation that demonstrates and teaches kingdom culture? How would that look? Let's look at some numbers. With only 1 out of 5 people in churches tithing or the average person in churches giving less than 2% of their income, evangelical churches in America still bring in an estimated $80B a year in income. With the kingdom of God and His provision demonstrated and taught, like Moses did, like Nehemiah did, like in Haggai and Joel, do you think it's possible to go from 1 of 5 tithing to 2 of 5? If people are transformed, aligned with the purpose of God in their lives and seeing His provision, do you think it's possible that people would flow or release instead of just 2% of their income, say 4%? Here's what that would look like.

Gross Income 1 out of 5 people tithing = **$80 Billion**

$80B – $20B = **$60 Billion**
(Gross revenue – mortgage debt = Operating budget)

Gross Income 2 out of 5 people tithing = **$160 Billion**

Gross Income – Operating Budget = **$100 Billion**

Currently these churches have an estimated $20 Billion paid annually in mortgage debt. With the increase as described above, revenues would double from $80 Billion a year to $160 Billion a year. If the extra amount were applied straight to the principal of the mortgages, all these churches would be out of debt in 2 years. Once the churches are out of debt, we free up the $20 Billion annually that is not going to the banks to pay mortgages. It has been estimated that it takes $17 Billion to feed everyone on the planet for one year. The United Nations estimates a cost of $30 Billion annually to set up sustainable agricultural programs to end hunger globally. Either way, by freeing churches in America from debt, we could solve world hunger in 2 years.

But, more than that happens. Not only are our churches now freed from debt, they have double the income as well. Again, this is not a growth model but merely an economic model, which means the doubling of income, is not due to doubling the amount of people coming to church. There is no need to add additional infrastructure or capacity; no new staff, no increased utilities, etc.; so the operating budgets would remain the same. With $160 Billion coming in annually and an operating budget of $60 Billion, we have literally freed up **$100 Billion a year, every year** for ministry and outreach!

What do you think the ministry impact would be of feeding all the hungry of the world? Do you think the Muslim world would be open to the Gospel of the Kingdom if we went into those countries and didn't say a word, but just fed their poor? This is the kind of stuff that keeps me up at night, because it's achievable! This isn't even a stretch or expecting a miraculous transfer of wealth. The money is already there, already in the kingdom of God, we just give it to banks to pay interest on debt instead of funneling it through churches to do ministry.

Abundantly More

We talked about ending world hunger with just a marginal shift in the body of Christ through alignment with kingdom culture and releasing of a small amount of resources, but what else? What would it look like to have His kingdom here on earth as it is in heaven? Throughout this book, we have talked about aligning ourselves with the Great Commission. What if we achieved it in THIS generation?

A friend of mine, Mark Anderson, was asked to head up the Global Pastors Network after the passing of Dr. Bill Bright, the network's co-founder. Through a series of divine appointments, he founded an organization called Call2All. Call2All is a partnership of hundreds of the top mission agencies, denominations, and organizations in the world, including tens of thousands of Christian leaders, all working together and strategizing to complete the Great Commission in our generation.

When I first met Mark a number of years ago, I was awed by the vizion God had given Him for the actual completion of this monumental task. He was the first person I had met that talked about the Great Commission in practical terms with numbers and statistics. "639 unengaged, unreached people groups of over 150,000 in population exist in the world today", he shared with a small group of us gathered at a friend's house. What would it take to reach them?

At this point, God had been stirring some things in my heart and I had the model above for freeing up $100 Billion a year. After the meeting, I approached Mark and asked him what it would take financially to complete his vizion. He had shared about moving the base of Call2All from Kansas City to Kona and so he began with those numbers.

"No, Mark, the whole thing." I responded.

"Oh," he replied, "well to set up our school and begin training our staff it would be..."

I interjected, "No, Mark, the whole thing. What would it take to fulfill the Great Commission in our lifetime?"

He stepped back a bit and looked at me.

"Oh, you think like I do! Well, I'm not sure, what did you have in mind?"

I told him of the idea of freeing up $100 Billion a year. He stuttered, just a bit, which is very unlike Mark and said, "Well, that, that would go a long way in getting it done!" The fact of the matter is God has already begun forming the teams of strategists, leaders, pastors, missionaries, prayer warriors, businessmen and women, intercessors, worshippers and so many others. He is aligning their hearts, and their efforts toward the completion of this task. No one is yet definitive on the cost it would take to complete, but money will not be the issue! All potential estimates that I have heard are less than $100 Billion a year.

At the end of the last chapter we talked about what it would look like if people in our churches were free from debt. The average American family has 30% of their income going out monthly to pay debt payments on everything from credit cards and student loans, to mortgages. If, like in Exodus, like in Nehemiah, we taught our people about the kingdom and they tapped into it from a financial perspective and became debt free, that would free up an additional

$1.2 Trillion a year every year,

with no noticeable change in their current lifestyles. All of those resources could go to fund vizion, ministry, outreach, missions and whatever piece of the Great Commission God places on their hearts.

There are organizations, movements and groups of people uniting together to find out what it will actually take to complete the Great Commission. The experts who crunch the numbers and map out where the Gospel has been and where it's not, believe it is achievable within OUR lifetime. Could you imagine? Talk about an opportunity to partner with God, what if WE were the generation to complete the last command of Jesus and usher in His return?!?! May God fill our hearts with His heart for the world and gift us with a sense of urgency to partner with Him in this effort.

And this gospel of the kingdom will be
preached in the whole world as a testimony to
all nations, and then the end will come.

Matthew 24:14

Call to Action

One thing is needed for these dreams to become reality – action. If 10,000 churches in America committed to transformation, as detailed here, we would begin to make a difference. When we demonstrate and teach the kingdom in our lives, our families, our businesses and our communities, things will change. When 100,000 churches join with us, the tide will shift, unity will become more evident and the flow of resources will be incredible. But when one million churches, across the face of the earth, work together in honoring the final words of our Savior and proclaim the Gospel of the kingdom through our culture and our very lives, the task will be accomplished.

The last battle scene in the 'Lord of the Rings' trilogy is in the final moments of the last movie, the "Return of the King". The leader of the remnant of the kingdoms of men rallies the troops with a cry about not losing heart. Several tense moments go by as he fixes his gaze on the impending battle ahead. The hoards of the enemy have closed in around this tiny group. They are outnumbered by a hundred to one at least; and their end is certain. They will die together on this battlefield, a last stand against a formidable foe.

As their leader looks ahead, aware of what he is leading them into, a sudden peace comes across his face. It is not the peace of assured victory; it is not the peace of avoiding battle, or security or comfort. It is simply the peace that, though this be the end, the cause is just. Aragorn, at that moment, turns and looks back at his fellow warriors, his brothers, his friends with inexpressible calm and yet tears in his eyes. All had been evaluated, all had been done, and it boiled down to this moment where he reached deep within and found the reason outside of himself for which this moment, his life defined him. He looked back, visible transformation on this countenance and whispered two words...

"For Frodo"

...And then he charged forward.

We are the church, carrying the culture of the kingdom and called to occupy and possess the lands that God has given us. It is a call, to live outside the four walls of our comfort zones and take massive ground for God. It is a war cry! It is a call for us to go forth and occupy the land that He has given us. We need you! Will you join us?

For the nations...

For the Kingdom...

For His Glory...